Our House

For consultants, facilitators or OD specialists, a house's familiar image will help their clients see, think and feel ways to solving their business issues. No need for dry and hard-to-remember management schemas. The striking visual and active methods shown here deeply engage clients – they get it right away. The House and its 'Rooms' make sense to them, and they willingly start working with you.

The Our House model has many of these 'Rooms' where complex business issues are sorted into one area at a time. The focus, the mood and the process vary with each Room, and the author reveals an entirely original consulting process each time. Disciplined creativity begins: loosening the grip of the past in the Attic; testing business foundations in the Cellar; preparing a meal the customer would love in the Kitchen; suppliers, maintenance and low-hanging fruit in the Garden; the team's dirty washing in the Laundry; elimination and waste goes into the Toilet; frank talk and vision alignment take place at the Dining Table; big systems perspectives can be seen from the Balcony; analysis in the Study; conversation and connection in the Living Room.

The simplicity of the images of a House and its Rooms belies their frugality and their strength. In each Room, your clients are *put through* something demanding yet liberating. They see things differently and they see different things. *Our House* shows you how to succeed with simple action methods that are enlightening and strong.

Antony Williams, Ph.D., TEP, works with leadership, planning and people-related issues in organisations. He is accustomed to training OD departments in large companies, health services and universities. He consults to senior teams, and facilitates high-profile and street-wise groups of participants. Antony is the author of *The Passionate Technique, Forbidden Agendas* and *Visual and Active Supervision*. He is a director of Santo & Williams, an OD consulting firm (www.santoandwilliams.com).

Our House

Visual and Active Consulting

Second (Revised) Edition

Antony Williams
Illustrated by Nelle Pierce

LONDON AND NEW YORK

Second edition published 2020
by Routledge
2 Park Square, Milton Park, Abingdon, Oxon, OX14 4RN

and by Routledge
52 Vanderbilt Avenue, New York, NY 10017

Routledge is an imprint of the Taylor & Francis Group, an informa business

© 2020 Antony Williams

Illustrations © Nelle Pierce 2018

The right of Antony Williams to be identified as author of this work has been asserted by him in accordance with sections 77 and 78 of the Copyright, Designs and Patents Act 1988.

All rights reserved. No part of this book may be reprinted or reproduced or utilised in any form or by any electronic, mechanical, or other means, now known or hereafter invented, including photocopying and recording, or in any information storage or retrieval system, without permission in writing from the publishers.

Trademark notice: Product or corporate names may be trademarks or registered trademarks, and are used only for identification and explanation without intent to infringe.

First edition published by Routledge 2018

British Library Cataloguing-in-Publication Data
A catalogue record for this book is available from the British Library

Library of Congress Cataloging-in-Publication Data
Names: Williams, Antony, 1941- author.
Title: Our house : visual and active consulting / Antony Williams ; illustrated by Nelle Pierce.
Description: Second Edition. | New York : Routledge, 2020. | Revised edition of the author's Our house, 2018. | Includes index.
Identifiers: LCCN 2019017499| ISBN 9780367277673 (hardback) | ISBN 9780429297779 (ebk)
Subjects: LCSH: Organizational change. | Organizational behavior. | Organizational effectiveness.
Classification: LCC HD58.8 .W5425 2020 | DDC 658.4/063—dc23
LC record available at https://lccn.loc.gov/2019017499

ISBN: 978-0-367-27767-3 (hbk)
ISBN: 978-0-429-29777-9 (ebk)

Typeset in Sabon
by Swales & Willis, Exeter, Devon, UK

 Printed in the United Kingdom by Henry Ling Limited

For Catherine

Contents

Acknowledgements ix

1. The Front Door: a guided tour — 1
2. The Innovation Hub: refine, grow — 7
3. The Basement: test business foundations — 19
4. The Laundry: reform — 29
5. The Toilet: eliminate — 39
6. The Dining Room: align — 53
7. The Balcony: see — 67
8. The Living Room: understand — 89
9. The Study: clarify — 109
10. The Attic: remember — 127
11. Goodbye, Keep Going — 149

Index 151

Acknowledgements

Long ago, an anecdote recounted by my colleague Bernie Neville about a house sparked an idea that became, for Chris McLoughlin and me, the beginning of Our House. The frame held good, and in fifteen years I have renovated it many times, and added rooms to cover all manner of consulting and facilitation issues. A book was begun, and along came Maree Gladwyn; her acuity, patience, and sensibility luckily saw many unfortunate sentences and paragraphs die in my waste bin. More recently again, Jenny Postlethwaite's advice and critique helped me get serious about publication. Pippa Lee Dow, Leanne Habeeb, and Diana Jones have read parts of the document and given valued advice and support. I am indebted to Bob Dick, Nick Wolff and Jude Treder-Wolff for their generous critiques of the final draft. Colleagues in Switzerland, Finland and Germany over many years offered gracious hospitality and valuable international perspectives on Our House's emerging frame. Thank you. Illustrator Nelle Pierce worked ingeniously and tirelessly on the cover and the illustrations, turning a flat manuscript into a vibrant book. And all along the way, from that first sketch to what you are holding in your hands now, Catherine Santo has sifted ideas and added to them. She road-tested some of the Rooms with different categories of participants, and Our House is broader and better for it. But it's for more personal reasons that this book is dedicated to her. And where would a book so focused on Vitality be without my beloved children Elisabeth and Samuel? They've made this actual house, the one I'm sitting in right now, the one with real beds and dining tables and laundries and kitchens and halls and a dog such a joy – what larks!

Chapter 1

The Front Door

A guided tour

Are you an experienced internal or external OD consultant, a manager seeking to revitalise a team, or a facilitator looking for some new frameworks? Come in. Welcome. The methods and techniques of Our House can assist you, for this is a book about ways you can help your clients think about their business. Every process described here is designed to promote clarity, vitality and alignment for your client.

We all know what a house is, and what each room is for – we don't need bedrooms or kitchens or toilets explained to us. Now put a consulting issue, say 'systems perspective' into a suitable 'Room' – the Balcony – add a set of techniques specific to seeing systems and one's own part in them, and you

2 Our House: Visual and Active Consulting

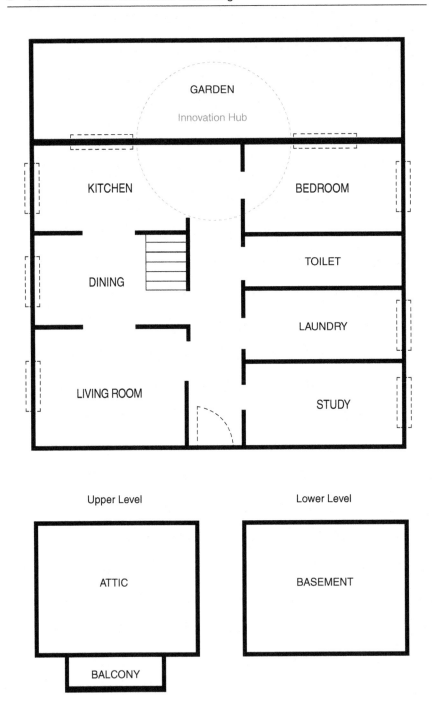

Figure 1.1 Floor plan

have already got one of the Rooms in Our House. A business frame and a set of novel techniques wait in each Room. Once you've seen the House, you can locate anything and remember everything: space gets laced with meaning, cognition becomes embodied, and clients get clear about their business.

You can start in whatever room suits your client's needs. Although the chapters are numbered, there is actually no sequence that must be followed. It depends on the job on hand. Start anywhere – Basement or Study or Balcony. The order is yours.

To help you choose, what if we have a guided tour ... let's go downstairs to the **Basement**, where work on foundations is done – there your clients test the very fabric of their business. The underground feel of the Basement – helped by pictures of columns, etc., indicates a step away from the day-to-day. But clients step away from the day-to-day only to reform the day-to-day by agreeing on the foundations of their business. They intensely examine these foundations for their adequacy and fitness to hold up the business above them.

Back to ground level now, and cross over to the right hand side. Here is the Study, the Laundry, and the Toilet. These Rooms engineer attention by having particular techniques proper to them, and may be just what your client is looking for. An exacting team performance self-review is offered in the **Study**. Other Rooms invite social and emotional response to a set of issues – in the **Toilet**, what to 'drop' (elimination issues of product, services or process), or in the **Laundry**, what to wash (structural, routine or delicate issues in teams). Being in a Room precludes other activities – all you can do in the Toilet is drop something or not drop something; all you can do in the Laundry is the washing. The very restrictions of the Room help teams be creative and stay on task, just as the restrictions of, say, ballet, intensify creativity, rather than reduce it.

On the left hand side of the House you will find the Living Room and the Dining Room. In the **Dining Room**, the focus is on the dining table, and the issue is vision and alignment to that vision. In the **Living Room**, clients use evocative figures to examine systemic issues within their organisation, and enter a peer consultation process.

The Rooms create their own emotional and intellectual climates. The mood and the work varies in each Room. Some Rooms have dreamlike, sexual or scatological overtones – the Bedroom and the Toilet are obvious candidates for this. Some, such as the Living Room, suit connection and reverie. Others, such as the Kitchen (where should we apply the heat?) and the Study (where are we strong and where are we weak as a team?), are fiercer. Unlike the cluster of Rooms in the Hub, which are run by a generic facilitation process, each of the other Rooms is specialised and has a unique consulting process attached. To my knowledge, this is the first time they have been published anywhere.

Including the Balcony and the Garden, there are nine Rooms in the House. It's best not to visit all of them in any one day. Indeed, sometimes much more than a day will be spent in just one room – I have several times spent three or four days in the Laundry with groups, just doing the washing. That room can open urgent issues of leadership, role clarity, organisational structure and team morale for inspection and repair.

Up the stairs is the **Attic** where clients can ease the grip of organisational memory's hold on current functioning and workplace culture. The **Balcony** is also upstairs – this is where clients, usually in leadership positions, can leave the dance floor and see over the whole landscape. The height and distance of the Balcony allows them to take a systemic view of their organisation, and their part in it.

Looking again at the floor plan, you will see that the **Innovation Hub** is at the end of the hall, opening on to the Garden, the Kitchen and the Bedroom. Unlike all the other Rooms we have encountered, these three – Garden, Kitchen and Bedroom – are run simultaneously by a single facilitator/consultant. If innovation is your brief, the three-Room Hub is an exciting place to work.

Except for the three Rooms in the Hub, I have provided a suite of tools, mostly involving action methods – physical and visual depictions – for each Room. But the tools are not the Room – they are merely suggested methods. We experience rooms in any house physically and symbolically. They have meanings and memories attached to them. The secret of Our House consulting is the metaphor of the Rooms themselves, and the use of the very simplest of action methods: stage, place, encounter, role, lines, objects, image and movement – to help business thinking. Issues unfurl towards the light becoming clearer, sharper and brighter. Solutions surface that were not seen before. With action methods, you see things differently, and you see different things.

The quaint domesticity of the Rooms is but a light cloak thrown over a hard-angled structure. Their apparent whimsy and innocence only intensifies clarity and the choices your clients must make. The aim is to deepen your practice and invigorate your organisational interventions. While the methods may appear jejune to your clients before you start, they are not so slight once participants are inside. With action methods, clients are always **put through** something. Participants are not observers – they are players, making choices and standing by them.

As you start to practise, you will appreciate more from the inside the hidden forces of the intervention you have chosen and the Room in which it is set. You'll get a feel for the basic chemistry of action methods – what interacts with what, what binds, what enriches, what soothes, and what transcends. If you work with your clients inside some of these Rooms for a while, following the set-ups as given here, you'll soon be able to improvise and adapt the work to your own style.

Having a feel for the Rooms, and for the action methods that can be used in them, will give you more joy with the designs you make, more ease with the processes you lead and more pride about your clients' outcomes as you lead them to clarity, vitality and alignment.

Facilitator, consultant, change agent, manager, organisational developer?

For simplicity's sake, I have called the person taking clients through the House 'the Consultant'. Some Rooms, such as those in the Innovation Hub, are consultant-light and facilitator-heavy, but with most it is the other way round. Since a lot of the teaching is done through 'cases', I have tried to avoid confusions of 'who's-who?' by having the Consultant's name always begin with 'C' – Clive, Corinne, Claude, Casey etc., and managers' names nearly always begin with 'M' – Max, Martin, Marina, Madeline and so forth.

Confidentiality, privacy

To keep confidentiality and help misidentify the workplace, sometimes these C men and women are the author, and often they are not. The Martins and Madelines and Marinas in the narrative likewise have identity makeovers. If they read this, I hope that their disguise is so heavy that they do not even recognise themselves. Their very workplaces have sometimes been spinally fused with someone else's. These graftings make it likely that our former participants cannot pick out their own organisations, far less anyone else's. The stories that I tell are told for illustration of a technique, rather than a journalistic reporting of an event. The point is to make it easy to use the House, the Rooms, and the process in your work with clients.

Chapter 2

The Innovation Hub
Refine, grow

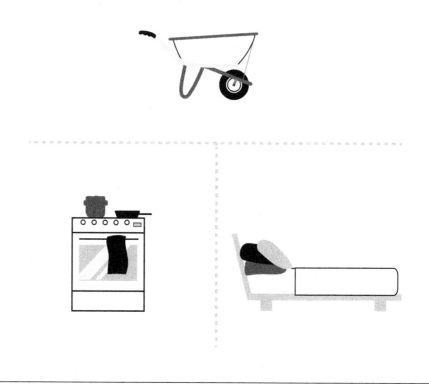

Three Rooms have been chosen here to show you the Innovation Hub – the Kitchen, the Bedroom and the Garden.

Part of our evolutionary story is efficiency: to save energy, we take shortcuts by privileging succesful ways of doing a task, 'routinising' it, and smoothing the neural pathways to and from it. This generally works well and uses less energy next time. It leads to us supporting habitual ways of perceiving the world, and dismissing anything that contradicts it. We really need our brains to do this work, or we would take forever just to make a cup of tea. But sometimes our energy-saving tracks do their job too well.

To perceive things differently, we need to create differences that are notable – that are 'newsworthy' in the brain. We have, somehow, to entice ourselves to move beyond our habitual efficient thinking patterns. One way of doing this is to pepper the brain with concepts or juxtapositions it has never before encountered. Using an analogue of transformation in a kitchen to transformation in a company makes one not only see differently, but see different things. We interrupt the normal flow of ideas, and create disruptive churn. Getting one thing – weeding a garden, say, to link with another – weeding a company, is the basis of work in the Hub.

The Firm that Couldn't Grow

Martin Hubbard's well-worn office was on the top floor of a corrugated iron building overlooking a belching paint plant. Trucks and forklifts circled it, like horsemen in an old movie circle a wagon train. From time to time, a mournful siren would go off in the plant. Martin was Sales Director at Pylon Paints.

Casey knew these siren sounds well. She had worked with other clients at Pylon, but never with Martin. He had phoned her out of the blue to ask her to run a two-day workshop on innovation with his entire Sales and office staff.

Pylon had its own Marketing division and a sophisticated R&D section populated by PhD chemists and engineers. That meant that Casey was dealing with a company that invested millions each year on innovation; it had an army of people whose sole job it was to invent and test new products or improvements to existing products. It had another, smaller, army devoted to marketing those products. Nevertheless, Casey was confident that if she used the Innovation Hub, she could get some good results – not necessarily new products, but perhaps helpful modifications in internal processes, customer personalisation, online services, and so on.

Martin told Casey that Pylon had been instructed by its UK parent to 'grow', and he was happy to try. He did not mind whether Sales grew market share, or simply cut internal costs, or both. The overall effect could be growth through higher productivity or through selling more product.

Casey briefly described the Our House metaphor and told Martin about her Innovation Hub plan using three Rooms simultaneously to provide three distinct lenses on innovation.

She asked Martin to attend the opening on Day 1, and the final hour on Day 2 when results would be presented to him. She said that it was very likely that the groups would be highly warmed up and keen for him to approve of their output in their presentations to him, and he might be sensitive to this.

Figure 2.1   Innovation Hub floor plan

Innovation efforts lose punch because the boundaries of decision-making are not set, and people wander in directions that will never be allowed by the company. Exhortations to 'think outside the box' are frustrating if company policy is actually bound by boxes within which decisions must live. It is not helpful for a group to work all day only to find that their solution is embargoed from the outset, and that it might, for example, require regulatory approval over which the company has no control. That is why Casey got from Martin a clearly articulated statement on the boundaries and budget limits of the project.

Reader, if you are going to work in the Innovation Hub, your sponsor, unlike Martin, may not be able to provide such a prior meeting, nor may they see their way clear to the intensive pre-workshop consulting process that Casey and Martin engaged in. In this case, you may have to make all your processes – "Short Form" – on the actual workshop day.

Here is Casey's plan for conducting the Long Form of the Innovation Hub.

Hub instruction, Long Form

1. **Identify the problem** – Martin 'owns' the agenda and introduces Casey.
2. **State the 'bookends'** – Limitations of company policy, taxation and legal limits, financial ceiling if the new product or process will cost, etc.
3. **Know the pragmatics** – How many people will be participating? Standard practice is to have three Rooms (including the Garden). If

your numbers are large, double the Rooms (e.g. two Kitchens, two Bedrooms, etc., or add a new Room, such as the Dining Room. The instructions for spin-off are the same as described below, and you can get the group to make up the similes). Figure on having 6+ persons per Room for a good vibe. Know what sort of working space you will have – this will affect your design. For example, are there breakout rooms or will participants all be in corners of the one large conference-style room?

4. **Introduce the model** – Present to the whole group about how the day will be run, that is, in a 'House' with three or four 'Rooms': Kitchen, Bedroom and Garden, in this instance, and roughly what happens there. Draw a picture of the Hub.

5. **Allocate participants to Rooms** – Casey divided the whole of Sales into three – about ten per Room. In one of their meetings she had worked with Martin to arrange the groups in ways that would provide the maximum diversity.

6. **People physically move into their allocated space** (10 minutes) – Still working in the large conference room, and using the list that she and Martin prepared, Casey gets people to move according to which Room they have been allocated. She points to various spots – 'Bedroom here, Kitchen there and Garden over there.' When people are in their place, she begins the warm-up to the individual Rooms.

7. **Warm-up to the Rooms** (about 30 minutes) – Still in the large group space so everyone can hear, she conducts rapid-fire warm-ups to each room, i.e. characteristics of a garden, what happens in a kitchen, to what do they associate a bedroom, and so on. See later in this chapter an expanded version of these warm-ups when each Room is individually portrayed.

8. **Homework** – She gives each group homework assignments, urging them to kick off from, say, intimacy in the Bedroom to how intimacy might apply to the business and to customers. If they are Kitchen people, what might it mean to apply the heat to something in their practice. Again, see the expanded version with specifics for each Room. She gives each person a set of note cards and asks them to write their ideas on these and bring them to the workshop in a fortnight.

Intermediate time between briefing and workshop day (where applicable)

9. **Reading and research** – Each person learns as much about the problem and solutions, if any, that have been tried elsewhere. Members are encouraged to look further, e.g. interview, read, web search, etc.

10. **Personal immersion** – Each member individually writes ideas on small cards, one idea per card. In the day's workshop, these ideas will be pinned up or stuck with magnets to a whiteboard. The cards are not signed, so that choosing a promising card to spend time on is done for the idea on the card, rather than the person's popularity or status.

On the day – morning session

11. **Pool ideas** – Once in their breakout rooms, individuals come together and display their ideas on a whiteboard or corkboard. Initial anonymity is desirable, but not mandatory. Emphasis is on the idea, rather than the author. Of course, other ideas can continuously be added throughout the morning as participants lever off each other, disputing, supporting, and critiquing.
12. **Dissent and debate** – The group rigorously tests possibilities and disputes the solutions put forward. In the process they bring up new ideas, which are also debated.

Afternoon session

Participants spend the early part of the afternoon selecting the best ideas and subjecting their productions to a more detailed and stringent examination.

13. **Solutions and evaluation** – Occupants of each Room select the best, most robust, and most fecund ideas. The consultant gets them to prepare a 'pitch' for their best ideas (30 minutes). The energy level is high for this, as the group will be competing with groups in the other Rooms to get their ideas launched. Paddle it along. People are deeply immersed in the products of their own rooms, and want to give detailed explanations to their peers of their virtues. Limit this discussion, but be sensitive – high ownership has built throughout the day.
14. **The pitch** – The ideas are presented to the senior manager, who can accept all or only some of the proposed innovations. The proposals are taken back to the workplace and feasibility studies are done.
15. **The fate** – Within a fortnight, if possible, the whole group reconvenes and participants are informed about which ideas were accepted outright, which were assigned for further research, and which were rejected. It is important to do this quite soon after the workshop. That way, morale remains high, even with those whose ideas were rejected.

Innovation Hub instruction – Short Form

This description of the Short Form relies on the more detailed description of the Long Form. The main difference from the Long Form is the lack of long-range preparation that participants have, and the prior allocation or

otherwise of participants to a particular Room, and therefore the composition of the group in any one Room.

Steps 1–7, with special care for Step 7, need to be completed on the morning of the 1-day workshop. The long Form version is certainly more powerful and better researched than the Short Form, but my colleagues and I have run several very successful 1-day Short Form innovation workshops. If a consultant can persuade their client to sponsor the Long Form, all the better, but in the world of consulting/facilitation things do not always work out that way, and your client may not have budget or leeway for a two-day workshop.

Innovation Hub: the Kitchen – transformation, heat, feeding

The basic formula for work in the Innovation Hub is using activities that happen in a room of a house as similes for what might happen in a workplace. Take the kitchen activity of looking into the back of the fridge and finding brown nasties and what's gone mouldy. These can be signs of over-purchasing and under consuming. Apply this to the supply chain of an organisation or part of it. This simile alone could repay a Kitchen group's attention for some time. Where is our balance in this? What should we do? What are we making that too few customers want?

Casey starts with the Kitchen. She asks participants 'What is a kitchen for – what happens there?' Participants at first give mild-mannered answers such as 'cooking', 'warming things up', etc. She can raise ideas about the kitchen as a place of transformation, of alchemy – raw materials like flour and eggs are transformed into a cake that can be offered to customers.

She might also ask questions about preparing and serving a meal that customers would love, or sharing a meal with suppliers and industry bodies and colleagues. They can prepare meals that customers want now, or that customers may want – or be taught to want – in the future.

You can ask the question: 'What would a kitchen be like to you if you were a cabbage?'

Members warm up and start to give answers such as: 'I would be sliced with a slashing knife, I might be boiled, I could be stir fried in a very hot wok', and so on. This sort of talk allows the consultant to introduce the idea of a kitchen being a tough place, a proving ground of ideas, as well as a generator of them. In the kitchen, ingredients are subjected to extreme heat or extreme cold. They are forced to blend with other ingredients, and whirred around or mashed in a mortar until they do. It raises the question: 'Is there any part of our work that could be blended?' When fire is the talk, you can ask: 'Where should we apply the heat?' When cutting: 'What can we cut?' and so on. The group gets the idea quickly, and starts making analogies themselves:

> "Over-finessing – using a mortar and pestle when a blender would do and the client does not know and would not care about the difference", says one.
>
> "Under-perfecting – using a blender when the high-end client wants artisan work with full flavour brought about by mortar and pestle," says another. They are away!

When you are convinced that participants have 'got it', move to the next room – the Garden, and start a similar exercise.

Innovation Hub: the Garden – low-hanging fruit, suppliers, pruning

'Innovation begins by observing customers' is an old saying (in innovation circles). There is another old saying: 'If you want to build a path, watch where people walk, then build the path.' As nature finds the easiest way to do things, find the way of nature. In the Garden, we find the way of nature, by growing things, and we find ways to thwart 'too much nature', as in weeding or pruning, so that the bit of nature we are interested in may flourish.

Members of the Garden group have heard your interaction with the Kitchen people, and are completely with you when you start talking about using a simile, say weeding, to generate ideas for their business unit. This means you can work more rapidly with them than you did with the colleagues in the first room. You ask the group 'What would "weeding" mean in a business unit?' This immediately opens up participants with some ideas – stay with weeding for a minute or two, asking a scattering of people. Then ask for something else about a garden, fertilising, say, accept it, and ask for associations with business training, leadership, rewards? Again, in rapid fire, collect some thoughts from two or three members. Move to pruning: one prunes for shape or for yield – how might that advance our organisation? You might ask: 'How would you sweep the paths to the customers' door?' and again quite quickly the group comes up with product ideas for external customers, or process improvements for internal customers. What about low-hanging fruit? Where are the easy pickings? Get a list up of garden activities (no need to ask for the business equivalent each time), and write them on a whiteboard.

Tell the Garden group that soon you will set them loose for a couple of hours to burnish the analogues that might emerge. Move to the Bedroom.

Innovation Hub: the Bedroom – blue sky projects, dreaming

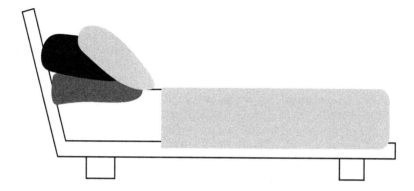

As in other rooms, your task is to get the group to free associate about the activities of the room. Since it is a bedroom we are in, you know that there will be nudging and laughter. Greet this with a straight face. You actually want sex and conception to be part of this room, but do not want the group to spend too much time laughing at the novelty of it. In the author's experience, work groups have a well-developed boundary with this type of material, and after the initial shock and laughter at the bedroom metaphor, do not breach that boundary.

Of course we know that a bedroom is a place for sex and conception, and that's one of the reasons why we are in this room in the first place. This certainly is a place for conception of new ideas. For example, you might reflect that conception takes two. If we were to conceive a new product, who – what company perhaps, or section of our own company – would have the best genes, would be the soundest parent for the long haul, would be the ideal partner? But as well as this, what happens in a bedroom? Participants call out items such as those below.

- Loyalty/commitment
- A place for rest and regeneration
- Dreaming – the unconscious rules, allowing new pattern making
- Dressing
- Looking in the mirror, drops, spots and all (laughter)
- Pillow talk – sharing information from the day
- Comfort and warmth

Because of its 'blue sky' nature, the Bedroom is possibly the most difficult Room in the Hub. Bedroomers are attempting to set the sights well beyond the current level of business activity. A Bedroom program has to maintain a fine line between productive lateral thinking, and uncritical brainstorming prolixity that quickly becomes sterile. Lean too far on the drive for closure, and the exercise loses what is best about it – the potential for opening up the unseen and unthought-of. Act too jocular and indifferent to outcome, and the group evolves from initial transgressive euphoria to boredom and passivity.

'*So, how could relationship loyalty and commitment translate to customer loyalty and commitment?*' Participants come forward with answers about commitment itself – how ordinary it is, how accepting of blemishes. What simple, concrete, little things build over months and years to a common anticipation and understanding of two parties? Some participants latch on to the notion that a parallel (definitely not sexual) daily kind of loyalty and commitment based on knowledge and tolerance might be possible with customers, and consider working on that during the morning.

Some troubles with traditional brainstorming

The practice of brainstorming was devised by Alex Osborn in the 1940s, and became one of the most widely used creativity techniques in the world. Amongst brainstorming's unchallengeable rules was that criticism and negative feedback were forbidden. If people were critical of each other, the process would fail due to 'evaluation apprehension' (fear of being judged by others). You had to be careful; creativity was construed as a delicate flower that bloomed only with praise. If people are frightened of saying the wrong thing, they'll not say anything at all, the theory went. Groups were urged to forget quality and focus on quantity. It didn't matter what one said, so long as one said something; in fact, many somethings.

The sad fact is that brainstorming consistently under-delivers. Decades of research have shown that members of brainstorming groups think of far fewer ideas than the same number of people who work alone and later pool their ideas. In a string of experiments, participants working on their own came up with roughly twice as many ideas as those in the brainstorming groups. To add salt to the wound, the solo workers' ideas were judged by a panel as more feasible and effective than those of the brainstormers. Brainstorming didn't so much unleash a group's potential as make individuals less effective. These research findings have done little, however, to dent brainstorming's popularity.

To counteract this, and working in the Long Form, Casey had people write ideas on cards, one idea per card, before coming to day two of the workshop day. The authors of the cards are unknown, and people arrange the cards into a hierarchy of ideas, not their proposers. Keep this part of the session short.

If you do conduct brainstorming in a group, it is desirable that the group in question is of mixed composition. There seems to be a certain point where too little comfort with one's fellows blocks creativity (too much newness and anxiety), but too squishy a comfort level ('we've all been together for years') also smothers it. Newcomers to a familiar group alter the mix and that very strangeness helps others to dig deep into the problem.

Other research found that debate and criticism, far from inhibiting ideas, stimulates them instead. In controlled studies, not only did the 'dispute and criticise' groups come up with more ideas around a given problem at the time, but they also had significantly more ideas some time **after** the experimental event. The process kept on going, it seems, like days-after flashes of scenes from a good movie. Dissent apparently leads to new ideas because it encourages us to engage more fully with others' work, and that makes us re-evaluate our own standpoints. Colliding perspectives seem to foster unconventional solutions to rocky challenges. The trade-off is that debate is less pleasant than agreement, and that one's feelings can be hurt when one's idea is pounced upon and dismembered. The Consultant who promotes lively debate cannot entirely prevent wounded feelings, but can establish a robust but respectful culture in the team, and certainly shut down attacks to the person.

Lastly, put your subject-matter experts together. They can suffocate the meek – people tend to defer to them and do not think of new solutions when they're around. In a group of their own, there's a chance that they will be their best and brightest selves in a similarly expert group. You will need them at wrap and critique time.

What does all this add up to? These counter-intuitive propositions, perhaps:

- Given the right atmosphere, criticism is more stimulating than inhibiting.
- Participants prepare ahead and write some ideas down on cards, one idea per card.
- A degree of strangeness (new members, odd members) seems to help.
- Groups should not be too small.
- Anonymous and even virtual groups can produce superior results, so long as members attend to the ideas of others.
- We're sharper and more productive when there is a small degree of social discomfort, and when we are challenged or our ideas criticised.
- Put your subject-matter experts together, rather than salt them through the groups.
- Organisational boundaries of invention or improvement should be known from the outset – what is possible, and what is ruled out.

Outcomes

Now it is time to briefly to return to Casey and Martin and the Firm that Couldn't Grow.

> Martin was an ideal receiver of the projects at the end of the day. He had a fine sense of theatre. All participants had worked hard to prepare their pitch to get it past their colleagues, and then to win approval from Martin. Martin had been in the Sales game a long time, and they knew they could not propose anything fluffy or thin to him. On Casey's advice, Martin sat with the head of Retail and the head of Trade at the closed end of a horseshoe, and the presenters stood with their posters at the open end. Casey has thus created a 'stage' to make the presentations more dramatic and interesting. A frisson was added to the process by each of the three 'judges' being seasoned veterans in Sales – they knew every spin there was to know, and the participants were quite aware of this.
>
> Nevertheless, the three hard-boiled bosses were amazed at the productions, and said so. Here are some of the outcomes:
>
> The groups made exceptional savings in internal processes. Though the notion of one's internal colleague being a 'customer' was far from new, seriously considering them as their focus in a two-day workshop paid handsomely in workplace dividends. Many redundancies were cut from internal processes.
>
> Martin thought the Bedroom group's ideas about customer loyalty, commitment and retention were well worthwhile developing. They were knocked back at Executive level, however, owing to clever lobbying by Marketing.
>
> Their one suggestion for product improvement was rejected by R&D.
>
> Thanks to the Garden group's ideas about 'sweeping the path to the gate' so external customers could get in more easily, small but useful improvements to the website and webpurchasing were adopted.
>
> After the workshop there was a marked improvement in culture both with the Sales and office staff. Relationships between Retail and Trade also improved from an already high base. At the next staff survey participants reported feeling they had more agency in the Division, more 'say' in what happened, and more understanding of the leadership required to get an innovation through the company, far less to market.

Chapter 3

The Basement

Test business foundations

Shaky foundations

Madeline stood at her office window, staring at the docks outside. The jostling maritime exterior, with its tugs, cranes and forklifts, seemed to bring her little comfort. Actually, these days, whenever Madeline looked at the view, instead of it restoring her, it worried her. These premises, in the most hip section of Liverpool's docklands, did not come cheap.

Madeline was the recently appointed director of a mid-sized consulting firm – Engage Consulting – in the north of England. She looked out at the industrious dock workers, and wondered aloud to Claude how Engage had managed to recruit so many staff who had started off working hard to win clients, and ended up with entitlement attitudes, short hours, long lunches, and a tendency to grandstand.

The firm had been making reasonable money in the good times, but was now slipping in the mild recession that was gripping the UK. Claude smelt damp and decay behind Engage Consulting's fashionable façade. Madeline told him that she could not understand how the firm retained any clients at all. The looseness of Engage's business model, the absence of anxiety about its diminishing fortunes, and the apparent indifference of its senior staff troubled her orderly, frugal heart.

Claude suggested to Madeline that the group start with the Foundations, and later work with three or four other Rooms. He described the Foundations process to her like this.

'We apply the metaphor of "foundations" – the concrete, steel or wood things that hold up a house – to the foundations of your company. When we've identified these foundations, we put their condition to the test. Are they strong enough, buried deep enough, close enough together to bear the weight of the house? Are they subject to damp, rot, or subsidence? In short, can they continue to support the place? Just as there's no point in renovating a house if one's foundations are weak, so there's no point in mounting a change program on cosmetic repairs. No matter how much re-plastering and repainting you do, ever more cracks appear, and the work has to start all over again. Does that make sense to you?'

Madeline looked relieved. She said that it indeed made sense.

I'll describe Claude's work with Engage at some length so you can get a better feel for the twists and turns of the process than you otherwise might through a recipe-like list. Such a list is attached a few pages down, however, and you can go straight to it if you wish. Here is an overview:

- Warm-up
- Team identification of 'the pillars of the business'
- Selection of pillars and reduction of alternatives
- Testing the four selected individual pillars for threats
- Working through threat reduction
- Re-testing the new pillars after a few months

Businesses fail when, over time, they do not manage 'the fundamentals'. A Foundations process in Our House is a back-to-basics one focusing on these fundamentals. Use it when you need to test the health of the supports for your clients' business.

In my work with companies over the years, I have often found that the main task in the Basement is not so much one of repairing foundations, but of actually finding them. This does not mean that they are not there – after all, if the business is afloat, they must be, or must have been. But they may never have been articulated, or are out of step for the business's changing context. So it was with Claude's work at Engage – the articulated 'foundations' were numerous and diffuse; some seemed to have little connection with running a business.

Warm-up

Claude's first task was to get the staff warmed up to house foundations in general, and later to foundations of a business. He drew a picture of a house, and underneath it the foundations, depicted as strong vertical pillars. He said that the foundations must hold up the house so that it doesn't wobble, lean, or collapse. In a similar manner to Casey's work at Pylon, but much more briefly, he asked what were some of the features of house foundations, and what can go wrong with them.

Selection of pillars and reduction of alternatives

When Claude considered that the participants had sufficiently switched on to the idea of foundations (that they should be enduring, strong, hold the house up, etc.), he said: *'Imagine there are four pillars that make up the foundations of this house – Engage Consulting. They're holding the whole thing up – or they should be. What are these four things?'*

The consulting staff comprised about 15 participants. Claude set them to work in three small groups, canvassing the 'foundations' of their business – what enabled it to stay above ground without collapsing.

While people went about their task, Claude taped a long thin sheet of paper on each of the four walls of the room they were in.

After about 40 minutes, participants came up with a list of 17 items – far too many. This spread of ideas, though, is not unusual in small companies that have put on staff piecemeal as the market demand grows. Claude had them reduce the 17 to 10 (there was much complaint), and then the 10 to 4. These were:

Experiential processes
Partnering
Cash flow – no debt
Shared theory

Developing the nominated pillars

To Claude, the participants' adopted foundations, even when reduced to four, seemed inward-focused and hardly a strong base for a business. They felt decidedly shaky. Yet he had to keep in mind that Engage, though in trouble now, had operated successfully for ten years. They must have at least an implicit model that had kept them in work.

Claude decided to re-work the newly selected four into foundations that might be strong enough for the job. He began from an Appreciative Inquiry stance, getting members to relate their successful uses of the 'Experiential Processes' with companies. Next he initiated a 'Foundation Inspection' process. This transformed the stylishly dressed consultants in the room into something a bit grittier: structural engineers in hi-vis vests and clipboard-toting building inspectors (they did not actually dress up). Often, the very notion of being building inspectors and structural engineers is sufficient to put participants into an engineer-like mindset to tackle the basics of their business.

Claude said that the most common problems with shakey foundations were 'cracks, rot, white ants/termites, shallowness, water damage, thinness, and movement of the subsoil'. He wrote these words on each pillar, and had participants select the most relevant test for the pillar in front of which they were currently standing. After some discussion, participants chose 'cracks' for the Experiential Processes pillar.

By now, participants are mentally in a highly visual and drama-like space. They 'descend' into the Cellar. They stand next to the pillars. This is hugely different from sitting around a table and discussing ideas. Drawing the pillars and having the group stand around one of them engages vision and begins a narrative – a story in which they are all involved simultaneously as

Figure 3.1 Foundations – four pillars

actors on a stage and as audience following the storyline. Vision is by far our most dominant sense.

More neurons in the human brain are devoted to vision than all the other sense modalities combined. Every day, we see colour, detect motion, identify shapes, estimate distance and speed, recognise faces, measure depth and judge the size of faraway objects. We fill in blind spots, and automatically correct distorted information.

Yet, although we might have plenty of PowerPoint presentations showing graphs and bar charts, we hardly ever use an image of a 'human-recognisable' object such as a pillar even when many firms talk of their 'foundations', or the four or five 'pillars' of their business.

Testing a single foundation – 'cracks'

Claude, still running a covert business model generation process, believes that at least one of Engage's business foundations must concern its 'value proposition' to customers: what does our customer need and how can we help? He put a few questions them along these lines:

What experience do we want our customers to have?
What are our customers' aspirations and how can we help them achieve those?
What are the customers' problems that this value proposition is attempting to solve?
Do our customers want a bundle of products and services that create value, or is it a single product?
Are we improving our customers' products or their performance?
Why do customers turn to Engage as against a rival firm?

After discussion, participants said that the 'crack' in Foundation #1 was one of definition and articulation. It was the gap between the customers' understanding of the offer and what the consultants thought they were offering. Experiential Processes was indeed their competitive edge, and their value proposition – rival firms offered 'off the shelf' programs that did not personally challenge participants. Clients stuck with Engage because it was personalised and challenging. They agreed to further define the 'Experiential Processes/Personal Confrontation' pillar so that each of them could articulate clearly what it meant, what the value to the customer was, and how it differed from rival offerings.

They had a long discussion on 'movement of the subsoil', and Madeline was at last able to find a receptive audience to take the recession – "movement in the subsoil" – in northern England seriously as a threat to Engage.

Testing another pillar – 'white ants'/termites

Participants excluded the pillar 'Shared Theory', when they found, after some work, that there were at least four 'theories' afloat in the company, and that even these were not in fact 'shared'. They installed a new pillar in its place – Relationship Marketing, since personal contact was the way in which they had so far got almost all of their business. Madeline worried that even relationship marketing – virtually their only strategy with a semblance of formality and discipline – had started to falter.

When asked to choose a threat to this pillar, they said that it had been 'white anted'. When Claude inquired 'By whom?', they answered that it was by themselves and the complacency that came with flush economic times. They weren't 'hungry' anymore because work came so easily and was so highly paid. There was also a rival firm – Sana Business Systems – white anting them. Sana had poached a couple of their young and most energetic consultants, and stolen one of their big clients. Claude started to build the idea that Sana was a kind of 'common enemy' eating away at their house from underneath.

The 'common enemy effect' is well documented in economics, game theory and psychology; it maintains that groups tend to bind together more strongly when they feel there is a common enemy to be protected against. It leads to development of an in-group 'us' and an out-group 'them'.

Participants agreed to have a day-long seminar on relationship marketing, and invite a leading CRM figure to present. They could keep their informal ways of relationship marketing, but realised that even such an apparently informal process needed consistency, sophistication and discipline.

'Positive cash flow' did not escape the newly fledged building inspectors. They found that it was a very popular pillar, but it was actually more of a goal than a foundation. They worked on Engage's revenue streams, customer segmentation, costs to the business and relative cost of resources. To Madeline's relief, they included the cost of running their office in one of the most expensive parts of Liverpool.

An action methods examination of one of the foundations

You may remember that the group claimed that 'Partnering' was central to its work – it had been Pillar #2. Claude had been hoping that 'partnering' referred to customers/clients, and would thus be an outward-facing foundation. He asked what partnering meant to them, and how it was manifested in Engage. They said it meant, 'sharing work' – working together with colleagues in the firm was 'very important'. They said that they frequently worked together, and were enriched by so doing. There was something unconvincing about these protestations, however. Claude was doubtful if this is how they actually went out on a job, and doubtful whether, even if they did back-office work in pairs or groups, it could be a credible 'foundation' for a business.

He decided to test their avowals by a spatial use of action methods (Williams 1989, 1991, 1995). He stuck a length of masking tape on the floor, and said that one pole represented 'Working alone every day in the past week' and the other 'Working with others every day in the past week'. He labelled one end 'Alone' and the other 'With Others'.

One at a time, each employee came out and stood at the place on the alone/with others continuum that best represented their actual practice. Their colleagues, who knew them well, could quiz the person standing on the grid if they thought they were inflating their frequency of partnering. To their own surprise, almost every person placed themselves high on the 'working alone' end. Claude changed the criterion from 'past week' to 'past month' and the frequency of co-work changed only slightly – apparently none of them actually worked much with others, even though 'partnering' was meant to be a Foundation.

Advantage of using even a modest visual and active method

The continuum described above is surely a modest form of action methods. Yet, had Claude not asked people to stand at various points on the line representing their practice, the discussion might well have gone on all morning. At least now the shocked participants had evidence, produced by themselves, that neither they nor their colleagues often 'worked with others' no matter how they greatly esteemed the practice. One side of the discussion was now anchored in daily life. Long story short, they found a new, externally focussed, emphasis in 'partnering' – it was involving the clients as partners, and being able to go for big jobs in pairs or threes.

The details and further workings of their resolutions are not our job here. The point is to illustrate that this simple device of using a continuum, making it concrete by a tape on the floor, and getting participants to stand at a point on it, is a part of the action methods toolkit. It requires very little upskilling for any competent consultant/facilitator. Yet, despite its modest facilitating demands, it brings with it the consulting ideals espoused in this book of clarity, vitality and alignment: it's clear, it's lively, and it helps clients align with each other and their leaders.

Figure 3.2 Working alone/working with others

A few months after these sessions, where participants had gone from 17 unexamined 'foundations' to a very tough four, Madeline told Claude that it had been the most valuable intervention the company had experienced in all her time as CEO. Engage staff's sincerely held fancies about how they worked were laid bare, and they good humouredly acknowledged their illusions, such as 'working together', and doing so on 'shared theory'. They deeply understood that the high economic times were over, and they needed to re-form into a tighter, yet more flexible unit. The 17 ideals had been not actually true to their daily work practices, and were getting in the way of recruiting new clients and retaining old ones. The four new foundations were stronger and more earthy. The sense of having a 'common enemy' had helped galvanize them into action, and they now approached their work with much greater urgency, tenacity and efficiency. Madeline and Claude started to plan work in other Rooms.

Summary of a Basement process

1. Draw a crude house on a whiteboard showing pillar-like foundations underneath.
2. Ask the group to relate to the notion of foundations holding up a house, and what can happen if these are inadequate or faulty.
3. Get the whole group together, or divide it if it is large, to work on three to five foundations of their own company. Keeping the number low concentrates thinking, and stops participants spraying conventional values and 'strengths' that the organisation may actually not have or need.
4. If the output is too large, help them reduce the numbers to the number of pillars you have nominated. You will have your favourite way of sieving complex data in a group to make it legible – voting, sticky dots, etc.
5. Produce long, thin posters for each of your nominated number of pillars. Stick them reasonably high up, so that people can read what is on them. The height also increases the dramatic basement-like element: looking up gives the sense of standing below ground with the foundations around them, and the house (which is their business) above them. The height and theatricality of the process changes thinking, and greatly assists investigating the pillars for faults.
6. Label each pillar with the title given by the group, e.g. 'Shared Theory', 'Value for Money' etc.
7. Stand with the group under the first pillar, and start to investigate its adequacy and health. Milk the metaphor, testing each one for the defect of your choice – white ants/termites, rot, obsolescence, weakness, etc. The metaphor salts a standard business development framework with

fresh thinking. When you have settled on a defect, say, 'white ants'/termites, you can follow down with your tests on the image.
a. *What are white ants/termites in this company?*
b. *Are they connected to company morale, poor team dynamics or rivals taking territory?*
c. *How long have they been gnawing away at the foundations.*
d. *Are the ants/termites inside or outside the organisation?*
e. *What is a remedy for these white ants/termites? And so on.*

The macro here is: use the metaphor to provoke new thinking, and then switch to the pragmatics of the actual business.

References

Williams, A. (1989). *The passionate technique.* London: Routledge.
Williams, A. (1991). *Forbidden agendas.* London: Routledge.
Williams, A. (1995). *Visual and active supervision.* New York: Norton.

Chapter 4

The Laundry
Reform

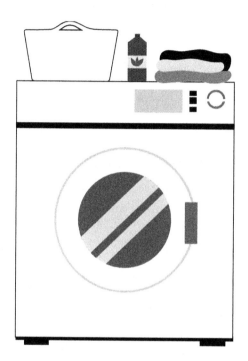

When to use the Laundry

When team members are not working cordially with each other – in open hostility, stony silence or destructive politics – their performance suffers.

Teams in difficulties often find it hard to speak openly about what is going on. Only some people, the loquacious ones, speak; others, the silent ones, hold their (non) peace.

This is where the Laundry Program can be useful.

In this chapter, 'sorting one's washing' is used as a metaphor for revealing difficult issues in a team. After an elaborate warm-up, members are asked to write an item on each of three cards representing three categories of 'washing' – Heavy Soil, Regular Wash and Delicates. The items are then separated into three 'laundry baskets', and the team works on the items one by one.

Quite apart from the unusual methodology, the process differs from a conventional 'team communication' process in that it allows members to surface troubling structural and leadership issues as well as interpersonal ones. It is not assumed that every problem is a matter of communication or team relations. The 'washing' to be sorted can include leadership, vision, structure, staffing levels, culture, and even the external financial and civil environment.

The Laundry process: 1. Warm-up

Ask each team member (for a team up to 14) how he or she sorts their washing at home. For example, Adrian says: 'Lights and darks.' Marcia says: 'I don't; my husband does it' (Laughter). Guang says: 'Lights, darks, delicates and towels.' Les says: 'Same as Adrian, but work clothes and socks are done separately.' And so on.

Believe it or not, the variety in how people sort their washing is of absorbing interest to their colleagues. I also ask, but not every time, 'Front loader or top loader?' and we might have a little discussion of the merits of front loaders, with me camping up a preference for one type (a front loader) and tut tutting those who have top loaders. I might even ask what brand their washing machine is. The lightness of this warm-up and discussion is justified by the task: you are using the Laundry Program because members of this group have difficulties with each other or with the organisation. They need to feel safe enough to be able to do what you are going to ask them to do: to sort the team's 'laundry', and then to start 'washing' various items – refreshing, repairing or making good. It gets quite serious quite quickly.

Note: in a highly acrimonious group, you might change the sorting warm-up from a 'sorting your laundry' to a more impersonal 'sorting laundry'. The sorting washing metaphor is only a vehicle for getting a team into the zone – alert, relaxed and creatively oriented to address its issues. Use your judgment. It is pointless to employ a warm-up of which you are enamoured only to find that you have shut participants down and created tensions about privacy or the separation of domestic and business life. I have never found this warm-up not to work, but once or twice I have diluted it for a group on the edge.

Instructions to the group

When the how-I-sort-my-washing warm-up is complete (20+ minutes – take your time and allow the group to relax), tell the team that today they are going to sort the team's washing into three baskets – Heavy Soil, Regular Wash and

Figure 4.1   Laundry – labelled baskets

Delicates. Give examples of what you mean by each, in the organisational context (see a list of some examples below) and hand out three cards, each a different colour, to each person. If you have drawn the baskets on a whiteboard, make sure that you colour code them, for example, red card/red basket matches for Heavy Soil, green card/green basket for Regular Wash, and yellow for Delicates. The cards do not have to be red, yellow and green, of course; they can be any three colours, so long as they are different from each other.

The example list below refers to team process, but if you are interested in using the Laundry for products, provide – or better, get the group to provide – equivalent suggestions for Heavy Soil, Regular Wash and Delicates.

Unlike other programs in Our House, you are not going to eliminate anything (the Toilet), and you are not going to invent anything (go to the Innovation Hub for that). The Laundry is a freshen-up, make-things-new-again program. You wash an item, and it is clean again, good as new, ready to wear or use.

Examples of Heavy Soil

Generally, structures and systems that are inappropriate and cut across the work find their place in this basket. Items might include:

> Issues with leadership at team level or above
> System-wide difficulties with change and adaptability
> Debilitating inter-team conflict or misalignment
> Poor role clarity
> Significant problems related to external relationships
> Lack of direction, foresight, 'vision'
> Hostility to innovation
> Split in the organisation/team
> Uneven workload

Examples of Regular Wash

Generally, slippages in good team practices, meetings, punctuality, performance reviews and so on get sorted to this basket. Might include:

> Problems related to team focus
> Lack of adequate meetings or forums for discussion/communication
> Difficulties in coping with setbacks
> Unpunctuality
> People not preparing for meetings
> Meetings not starting/ending on time, minutes not taken, actions not followed up
> Lack of an effective team scorecard process
> Duplication, re-work. Tasks get done twice or more

Examples of Delicates

Generally, apparently insignificant matters that cause distress and are extremely hard to talk about are here. They might include:

> Problems related to internal relationships
> Interpersonal member–member conflicts
> Rudeness, abruptness, bullying
> Sensitive gender or age matters
> Disability
> Awkward personal habits etc.
> Communication challenges faced by virtual teams
> Problematic member–leader conflicts
> Micro management

As you can see, any one of these could be listed in a different basket – bullying could be a Delicate or it could get thrown into Heavy Soil. 'Difficulties in coping with setbacks' might be flung into any of the three baskets. Inability to manage oneself around the unspeakable and Super Delicate 'Awkward personal habits' could be the main reason why the team is in trouble. The point of this warm-up is to get the group talking about difficult issues when their past habit has been to remain silent about them. As I will stress below, the baskets and their categories, once they have been named, become irrelevant, and the items themselves can be 'clouded' into themes – an 'affinity diagram', if you like.

Writing the items and placing the cards

Ask participants to write one Heavy Soil item on their red card, one Regular Wash item on their green card, and a Delicate item on the yellow card. Draw three baskets on a whiteboard, label them 'Regular Wash' etc., and have members place one of their cards 'in' each basket, attached by magnets or by self-adhesion if you are using Post-its. If a whiteboard is not available, you can also have three small tables out the front, labelled appropriately, but note that items flat on a table are a little more difficult to read when there is a crowd of people hunched over them. After the cards are placed, invite team members out front to read all the cards in the three baskets (about 5–10 minutes). Then they return to the circle and sit down.

Once this process of writing and reading is complete, you may sense a relief – a kind of group sigh and stretch. This can be especially so if the team has been suffering constant conflict, and has split into dysfunctional factions. Factions, alliances and coalitions are a natural part of human organisation, and are not always 'dysfunctional'. Problems associated with a team's ability to establish a clear direction and effectively organise itself to meet its business objectives are often as important contributors to team morale as the failure of internal relationships themselves, and can indeed often lead to such failures. In other words, it can be a mistake to attribute all poor performance to failure in internal relationships. Poor performance can come from many sources: how can one kick morale-boosting goals if one does not know where the goalposts are? The Heavy Soil basket can, and does, flush out structural and leadership problems. To repeat, the Laundry Program is not only about how we are getting on with each other, important though that be.

Working through the issues

The Consultant picks one of the cards (I often start with a card from Regular Wash), reads what is on it, and asks who wrote it. In this process, the Consultant makes it clear that there is no obligation for any individual to 'own' the selected card. I explain that it can be helpful so that what is in the

Figure 4.2 Laundry – labelled baskets with Post-its

text – a short sentence, usually, like 'Meetings are becoming almost a waste of time' – can be fleshed out by the author of the item. Because it is a Regular Wash card, and what is written is fairly innocuous, the writer is likely to acknowledge authorship. If he or she does not do so, however, I make a guess about what the meaning may be, and invite the group to do likewise: *'Mary, what do you think could be behind this card about meetings?' 'Ravin, what do you think the author meant?'* We then discuss the item.

Let us say that the selected Regular Wash item is 'Meetings are becoming almost a waste of time'. The author, Andy, is happy to come forward, and explain his intent when he wrote the card. Andy says that the group meetings do not follow proper meeting protocols; that few people prepare for them; that they wallow around in discussion, and rarely come to a decision, and if they do, it is not followed up. No times are set, and no particular person is made responsible for the action. The Consultant asks the group if other members share Andy's view of their meetings. In our example, many do. Given that this is a point of consensus, the consultant pauses on this item for some time, since it may be indicative of a lack of role clarity and purpose in the group that goes deeper than poor meeting habits. Can the members agree on what should be the case? In an ideal situation, they themselves may come up with better meeting protocols. If they do not, the Consultant might coach them. This discussion may take 45 minutes or more. During the discussion make sure that there is a note taker, action points and timelines – it is all too easy for a consultant unconsciously to follow the same pattern that he or she is attempting to reform, and to sink comfortably into the very 'wallowing' culture that Andy is describing.

In the discussion of matters arising from Andy's Regular Wash card, many of the other points that have been listed by group members (e.g., 'We don't take notes'; 'People come late'; 'There's no serious agenda') emerge naturally and do not need to be covered again. It is not desirable to take up every single point written on every card, given there is commonly a great deal of overlap. In a half-day session, one might read out and deal with just two or three of the cards.

Just before the first session finishes, I ask the group if I may take the cards back to my office and sort them into themes. I pledge that at our next meeting, I will present these themes, and show them the original cards too, so that they are sure the message on their card has not been airbrushed out. They like this idea. It respects the work they have done, and shows that it will be used in some way. They are relieved that they haven't spent yet another morning on material that goes nowhere.

The original baskets are now irrelevant – one person's 'Delicate' is another's 'Regular Wash'. The baskets have done their job in getting the team to nominate its issues. How those issues are then dealt with is up to the individual consultant and his or her favoured modes of working in business settings.

Mac's Disconnect – an example of a Laundry Program

You will have picked up that it does not greatly matter if people construe the categories differently. More importantly, under the Laundry Program, everyone becomes a contributor, and furthermore, they contribute not one but three items. It is the experience of many consultants that when there is 'trouble' in a group, the hardest thing is for the group to talk about it, and sometimes the most silent people are the most troubled by the trouble. When this method is used, they get a say, at least on a card. They usually go further; their tongues are loosened by the warm-up process, and by writing their issues. They do not seem to mind having their card read by all of their colleagues, as long as authorship does not have to be revealed. They are relieved when they find how similar their issues are to those of their colleagues.

Given the range of items and the mood of the team – relaxed vs tense – it matters what is on the first card to be read out. If members appear very anxious, perhaps fearing an explosion, a card such as 'More social interaction – drink after work, remember birthdays, etc.' at first apears to be a helpful one to read. Not only is the material likely to be less flammable, but in working through whether and how to have 'more social interaction, drinks etc.', members can get a sense of success and accomplishment – a 'runs on the board' feeling. Planning 'more social interaction – drinks after work etc.' is an apparently humble and benign place to start, but dangerous if it contained any apparent endorsement by you of the 'drinks after work' part of it (motor accidents and other horrors). Moreover, if the team is in very bad shape, the last thing that team members want is more social interaction. Your best bet for a safe start with a very troubled team is probably an 'Acknowledge group successes' item, if such a one exists (it often does, under various linguistic guises). This may settle participants into the process, and prepare them for more contentious items.

Once again, how the Consultant deals with the material depends on their consulting framework. Also relevant is the level of the team within the organisation. Some of the examples given are from teams fairly junior in the heirarchy, but it is strange how universal are the types of items and the utility of the Heavy Soil, Regular Wash and Delicates categories at any level within an organisation to get at 'what is going on'.

You could put a line of tape on the floor at this stage. Let's call it the 'Difficulty of Implementation' line. You can call one end "Hard to implement", and the other 'Easy to implement'. Then the criterion; we'll say in this case it is 'Acknowledge successes'. Now start the action process by inviting team members to stand on a spot on the line that represents how hard or easy it will be for this group and its leader to acknowledge successes. If there is enough psychological safety in the group at this stage to do so, you can interview each person on the line about why they are there.

Figure 4.3 Difficulty of implementation line

Or, you could draw on a whiteboard a four-box matrix, which would simultaneously show the difficulty of implementation against importance of the reform. Each person would make a mark with a sticker or whiteboard marker that reflected their view on the significance of the reform vs its difficulty. This is still more active and engaging than sitting in one's spot and commenting. If you want to raise the commitment stakes another notch, draw the matrix on the floor, and invite members to stand in a spot that represents their views. The Consultant interviews them on that spot about why they are there and not somewhere else.

A Laundry program, using advanced action methods

A small Finnish consulting and training organisation operating in two parts of the country (the 'Easts' and the 'Wests') were on a two-day Retreat. about 25 members were present. By day two it was clear that there were difficulties with administration, goal setting, standardisation and future directions. These difficulties had only obliquely been alluded to. Claude invited participants to the Laundry, conducted the sorting-the-washing warm-up, and distributed the different coloured cards as described already. When they were finished, they laid the cards on three separate tables, and walked around, inspecting each other's offerings.

Important, difficult to implement	Important, easy to implement
Not very important, hard to implement	Not very important, easy to implement

Figure 4.4 Difficulty of implementation matrix

Claude then gathered the cards and put them in three separate plastic buckets, with the colour on the outside of each bucket. The teams sat tight together, as befits a small space such as a laundry. Claude then asked the two business owners to go to the Heavy Soil bucket and select two cards that were of most interest to them. They did, and selected the cards that spoke of the potential split they were facing. They read them out loud to the group, and invited discussion. This came readily, with people pointing out difficulties and flaws in the organisation as it was currently set up. Note the departure from the normal process of selecting a Regular Wash item first, to allow the group to settle down. By this stage, however, the group had been together for a full day on the previous day, and had been involved in other operations. 'Settling down' was not an issue.

Claude then moved the group to the larger floor space and construed the difficulties as 'spots' or 'stains' on the garment of the organization. He asked the leaders to get cushions that would represent these various spots and stains. They did, and threw them on the floor with considerable heat, naming each one.

The question then was whether the organisation could launder the stains, given they were so prominent and apparently indelible. The two leaders asked for time out to talk, and the group had a long lunch break. After lunch, the leaders announced that there was no stain remover in the world that could remove the spots. There were irreconcilable differences in culture between the 'Easts' and the 'Wests', and that the groups had been growing further apart in the previous two years.

Members were greatly relieved that at last there would be a formal split, and spent some time discussing operational and financial issues.

The split was successful, and five years on, both parties are operating happily in their specialty.

The illustrations of the process detailed above concern team-based processes, but you may note that a Laundry program can also be used about a **product** that may be a little grubby – not needing to be thrown out, but simply washed and refreshed. To this extent, the Laundry can become one of the Rooms in the Innovation Hub, described earlier.

Summary of the Laundry process

Conduct a laundry warm-up by asking participants how they sort their actual washing at home.

Ask participants to sort their organisational 'washing' into three categories – Regular Wash, Heavy Soil and Delicates.

Participants write their concerns, one per basket, on diversely coloured cards.

They place the cards in 'laundry baskets' drawn on a whiteboard.

They read each others' cards and get an idea of the group's concerns.

Consultant selects one of the cards, reads it out, and members work through the issues on this card (30–60 minutes).

They resolve the issue.

Consultant selects another card and follows the same process.

Consultant pools the data into themes for the subsequent sessions.

Consultant works through the data with the participants in the next few weeks.

Chapter 5

The Toilet
Eliminate

Alliance's clutter: a product elimination program

As the new head of Alliance Stores, Jim Phelps often said 'No' to the offers and 'great ideas' that unspooled daily across his office.

On his desk, and facing the visitor, was a little sign:

Strategy is what you say NO to.

The first decisions in implementing a strategy usually concern what we want to create or enhance, and then only, sometime later, what we have to restrict or extinguish. But it is possible to start a strategy from the other end – with what you want to restrict or stop. In the Toilet Program, we focus exclusively on these. Thinking up something new is fun; deciding whether and how to abandon what does not work, seldom is. Attachment to 'the way things are' grows extra arms and sharp claws when we have to get rid of something. We clutch our obsolete processes, and we cling to no-longer-good products.

The discipline of innovation is less a brainstorm than a diagnostic: a systematic examination of areas of change that offer opportunities for growth and value. Growth comes from customer take-up, new products or services, and higher margins. Value comes from lower costs and increased speed.

The Innovation Hub does the first, and both the Hub and the Toilet Program grapple with these last: reducing costs and increasing speed by eliminating obstacles causing resistance and 'drag'. Our first case does not have an actual toilet depicted - a box matrix on a large whiteboard is used instead - it's the 'stage'. Manipulating magnetised images constitutes the action part. The Toilet is most commonly used for business processes, but this case illustrates product elimination.

> When Jim came into the job as head of Alliance, he was told that Alliance's problem was one of 'identity'. Prior to Jim's advent, the in-trouble company had done several retreats with various consulting companies focusing on mission/vision/values. Nothing had changed. Jim soon realised that the issues were not 'identity'.

A Toilet Program helps people see a picture that was always there to see, but could not be seen until a frame is provided. Mostly in this chapter we will be stressing the somewhat theatrical use of a simulated toilet – namely a chair with a waste bin beside it. But drama can come in many ways, and in Alliance's clutter it comes in the form of cut-out magnetised products of a furniture chain being consigned to the 'Reduce' or 'Eliminate' box of a four-box matrix. The aim, as always, is clarity, vitality and alignment.

> Consider the highly paid executives of Jim's new company, a company with a long history in mass-market retailing. They are experts in sales, supply chain, marketing, business models and operations. Yet, Alliance is going to the wall, because of what had become wallpaper – a pattern so familiar they could no longer see it.
>
> Alliance Stores had two main competitor chains: Bestway Family Comfort and My Castle. Both were doing better than Alliance. The question for Jim was not 'Who is Alliance?' as he had been told, but why did three companies exist with sales to similar demographics, and one (his) did not make money while the other two did.

Jim searched Alliance's inventory. He found that they stocked about 800 items, while the two rival chains stocked only about 500. Jim engaged his business analysts for a week of preparation, and hired some temps to assist them in producing data on every item sold by Alliance. He also visited each of Alliance's warehouses and investigated what was stored there, even though he could have relied on a computer inventory. He wanted to get the feel of each place, and the smell of each place. He found the warehouses were rather leisurely places of low activity – there's not much movement in a warehouse when sales are slow. He asked warehouse staff which items had been there for more than 6 months, and which had been there for even longer – 12 months or more. They knew their stock, and were able to tell him immediately.

At last Jim was ready for his Retreat – a different kind of retreat than that to which the managers had been accustomed. After introductions, Jim conducted the warm-up. It was pretty simple: he told them that this was a time to take a time-out, a step back, and 'a good hard look at what's going on'. He said that for the past ten years whatever it was they were doing, it hadn't worked, and that they would all, including himself, be out of a job if it continued.

From a whiteboard at the front of the room, he dramatically unveiled Kim and Mauborgne's (2005) simple grid – Raise, Create, Eliminate, Reduce.

He'd had one of his assistants produce pictures of every type of item sold (or more often, not sold) by Alliance. This was easy to do, as nearly every item for sale was illustrated in the quarterly catalogue that Alliance stuffed in letterboxes. The pictures were individually cut out from the catalogue, laminated, and glued to magnetic tape.

Eliminate	Raise
Loss-making items, especially big-ticket items	
Reduce	**Create**
Number of items overall by at least 25%	
Large items taking a lot of warehouse space	
25% of warehouses themselves (staff were to be redeployed)	
Over-rich choice for small electricals	

Figure 5.1 Simple grid emphasising the Reduce/Eliminate column

He picked up a magnetised picture of a freezer from the table beside him and slapped it on the 'Eliminate' box, and then moved it to the 'Reduce' box, and then back to Eliminate. He said,

This is what we are going to be doing for the next two days with each and every item we sell. We are not putting anything as yet in the right-hand (Raise/Create) column. That's for later . . . if there is a later.

Jim insisted that the group put all loss-making items – no matter what the cause – into the 'Eliminate' box. He did not do this for them, as he wanted them to pick up the items and walk to the board and put them in that box. This is a stronger and deeper action than simply observing that a large number of items were corralled in a box labelled 'Eliminate'. Jim himself could have done the whole job in his office, based on the data that his analysts had provided. But that would have meant that his executives were not part of the process, and that they would receive the news as 'an edict' from the new boss. They may have complied, but their compliance would not have come from a grounded understanding of how the business had to change.

The magnetised pictures could only be removed from the Eliminate box on the grounds of a strong argument (e.g. 'We do make a loss on this item, but it is a curiosity and brings people into the store who then buy other items'). Such arguments were challenged, initially by Jim, but later by the managers themselves. In most instances this type of argument ('Yes it makes a loss but it brings customers in who buy something else') were not supported by data, were thrown out, and the item stayed in the Eliminate box.

The management group, after their initial shock in keeping non-profit-making items in the 'Eliminate' box, had become sterner. They addressed big-ticket items that swamped warehouse space, such as fridges and outsize TVs. From Jim's weeks of preparation, they had three years of sales data provided on each of them, including store-by-store volume and profit margin. They did not eliminate these altogether, but put most of them in the 'Reduce' box. The executives were alarmed to discover that Alliance stocked 16 different kinds of home heaters; they cut them to 4 and put the remaining 12 into 'Eliminate'. They discovered another exotic line of large freezers, which again took massive warehouse space. All but two brands went into the 'Eliminate' box. They made plans to close two warehouses and retain five.

By focusing only on the Eliminate/Reduce side of the equation, Jim had been able to turn Alliance around, save the company, and the employees' jobs. When he had steadied Alliance in terms of costs, he could start looking at what he intended to raise and create. He was cautious in this, however, in the light of Alliance's hoarding history. He was disinclined to repeat the error of previous management groups that had focused on acquisition as a way out of trouble. This practice had led to the bizarre inventory discussed above.

A Toilet program for internal process minimisation

A Toilet Program is basically a matter of 'NO', of elimination. It can be used to say 'no' to all kinds of processes, products, partnerships and markets. It would be most disrespectful to use it for personnel reduction, and should NEVER be employed for that purpose. The most frequent call for it, in my experience, concerns organisational processes that are seen as petty and redundant. They are like the never-cleaned barnacles adhering to a ship under the waterline, growing imperceptibly, increasing the drag, slowing the ship. They're called 'prudent governance' by those who like them, and 'red tape' by those who don't.

Alliance's story concerned stock. There are many client organisations of the readers of this book that do not actually have or sell 'stock' – hospitals, government departments, universities and so on. These organisations do, however, have products and services, which are a form of 'stock' in some ways parallel to Alliance's. Like Alliance's large freezers or multiple brands of toasters, they tend to:

- take up 'room';
- take up time and tie up staff;
- be past their use-by date;
- have become 'invisible' – part of the wallpaper;
- be seemingly unwanted by anyone;
- be offered elsewhere in the organisation;
- be needlessly complicated;
- provide too many choices that compete with each other.

These factors are easy to disapprove of, and make the Toilet a popular destination in Our House. Executives, chafing too long under compliance's starched collars, leap for it. They cannot stand any more the petty forms, the fear-driven email inclusions, the constant meetings, travel clearance, payment authorisations, accommodation levels and reporting, reporting, reporting. They are thwarted by rigid adherence to occupational health and safety protocols. They want speed, and resent the fussy pit stops of compliance and the drag of rules. They despise 'red tape', which they see as the onerous edicts of minor functionaries. The thought of slashing red tape gives them an emotional charge. So it was with the executive group of BioChem, a large, publicly listed, international chemical company.

Biochem's jam

BioChem, one of the top 20 companies in the country, and a serious player in the world market, was languishing in the stock market, and seemed unable to lift its performance. The CEO had gathered his senior executive group for a two-day retreat to garner ideas, yet again, about how to remedy this situation.

A week in advance of the retreat, the 11 members of the Exec group received from me a rundown on Our House – a description of the Rooms, and how the Rooms could help them focus on a particular activity to the exclusion of all others. The Toilet was one of those Rooms, and Exec members were provided with a short description of the process. If they wanted to choose the Toilet as their preferred space for the first morning, they should prepare thoroughly and bring any relevant documentation, statistics, etc. that would help their work.

An advantage of working with a senior executive group in the Toilet is that there is enough firepower in the meeting to approve of virtually any change that members wanted to make – the CEO is there, the head of HR, the Chief Legal Officer, the COO, and so on. A Toilet Program can be completed and signed off within three hours without need for referral 'upstairs'. In this case, there is no 'upstairs'.

Set up the working space horseshoe-fashion with a half ring of chairs and no tables. At the open end of the horseshoe place a chair with a bin beside it, faintly suggestive of a toilet. The person proposing to eliminate a troublesome legislation sits on the focus chair, and holds up their item – a description of a process or product. The presenter advocates that it be dropped. They might even wave it provocatively over the bin and challenge other members to preserve it.

The Toilet group execs had done their homework and were clear about what they wanted. They had with them photocopies of tiresome legislation, admonitory emails, minutes of meetings, and so on. They argued that many of their processes and procedures were out of date and a drag on the system. Each of them thought that all of the others would quickly agree that their chosen items would be seen as redundant and should be rapidly eliminated. The group could then move on to the next item. Their rush to cut was soon dashed, however, when they discovered that the loathed regulation they had in their hand was brought in as a response to a theft, a court case, a harassment suit, a scandal, or even a death. With each of these, especially the last, procedures had become more tightly prescribed.

Organisational stories surrounding a despised regulation leap into life when attempts are made to choke or bury them. Someone in the group tells the others how the offending protocol was aimed at certain cowboys in the past who had tickled the till, rorted the system, or cut corners on safety and thus injured or killed someone. The old ones nod at the memory. To drop even the simplest and most obnoxious item is almost always a struggle, even with high-powered and impatient groups such as this one. Why is it so?

There are settings – 'status quo bias' – within each individual that baulk at change. Anxiety associated with the risks of engaging in something new, or becoming once again exposed to past dangers, often builds up and makes it easier for the person to block the change than to go with it. Striving to reduce anxiety, people engage in avoidance behaviours, hoping to keep themselves out of frightening situations. Every alternative to the otherwise nonsensical situation they are putting up with can appear more frightening than the lumpy status quo. Also playing a part in the freeze is fear of a 'narcissistic injury' – of having to acknowledge that the present state of affairs, over which one might have had some control – is deficient or outmoded. People will go to great lengths to preserve what to an outsider seems a dysfunctional way of operating. They put up with extremely inefficient and unsatisfactory impediments rather than improving their situation by taking on the risk, and stepping towards the unknown.

A Toilet Program has some possibility of success because it can crystallise discontent. The clarity brought about by the dramatic device of holding an item over the 'toilet' pushes the other participants to see more sharply when their fear is at play and makes it harder to deny that something must be done about the situation. Where members of a group interpret the avoidance as having anxiety at its base, they are more likely to have an 'aha' realisation.

> After their allotted three hours the BioChem group had made some progress, and got rid of a few items, but had run into pockets of conservatism, including their own, at every turn. They wondered aloud, 'Why on earth is this process so slow and so hard?'

Taking some concepts from the psychological and sociological literature, let us explore a little further possible answers to their question.

Status quo bias and regret avoidance

Any departure from the status quo risks touching a tripwire of psychological and social danger. 'Status quo bias', as its name suggests, is a preference for the current state of affairs over any other. Experiments in many fields have led to general acceptance of the phenomenon; in a typical experiment, subjects are divided into two groups, each of which has to make a decision in a variety of problems. One of the groups is told the status quo for each decision, and the other is not. The groups that are informed of the default positions overwhelmingly choose those options. The groups that were not informed of the default positions chose more or less randomly. Status quo bias also explains the preference for companies to devise opt-out plans, rather than opt-in plans. In an opt-out plan, one is automatically enrolled unless one asks to be excluded; people stay in – it seems easier and less risky. Their 'policy' rolls over every year, greatly to the utility or insurance company's delight.

The notion of 'regret avoidance' may also be useful here: people apparently load up the potential losses from switching away from the status quo more heavily than the potential gains. This makes it more likely that they will not switch at all. Staying with what worked in the past (or even, more simply, *existed* in the past) seems safer, easier and requiring of less mental effort than changing course. It seems that if things go wrong as a result of a decision we made, we regret having taken action more than we would have if we had done nothing. This impression – that it hurts more when we act and are wrong – is backed up by studies in neuroscience, which found that erroneous status quo rejections have a greater neural impact than erroneous status quo acceptances, especially in difficult decisions. Given all these factors, plus the powerful social impact of some members of a group over-emphasising the avoidance of loss, the status quo, no matter how apparently silly, is likely to be favoured, at the inconvenience of all. The positive consequences of gains are psychologically awarded less weight than the losses that might occur if the status quo were changed.

Altruistic punishers

Another helpful concept for understanding puzzling results in a Toilet Program directed at internal processes (remember, the Toilet is also useful for products, as we saw with 'Alliance's Clutter') is that of 'altruistic punishers'. Many pesky rules, restraints and checking systems in internal processes have been put there to foil skivers and cheats. To take a minor example, let us say that work-related travel costing more than $800 has to be cleared by a succession of team leaders and managers. Everyone knows that this limit is ridiculous, that it takes up people's time, slows things down and exasperates applicant and bureaucrat alike. When in a Toilet Program it is about to be dropped, however, there is a sudden outcry. A member directs the group's attention to certain notorious historical figures, since departed, who used to cheat on travel and goodness knows what else. The Moral-High-Ground button is pressed; the group's indignation expands like an airbag in a crash, as its courage shrinks. Members decide that 'for now' they will keep the $800 limit in place. To understand this reaction, so deep in the space of unproductive activity, it may be helpful to consider the notion of 'altruistic punishers'.

Why is it that people will put up with onerous over-regulation in an organisation for the sake of foiling a minor villain's efforts to cheat on travel claims? An interdisciplinary group of economists, anthropologists, biologists, psychologists and sociologists at MIT (Gintis et al. 2005) gathered data in controlled laboratory and field environments. They argued that a significant portion of people, instead of being simply selfish and materialistic, are 'conditional co-operators'. They will behave altruistically so long as others are doing so; they will co-operate until they realise others are not. This is the 'if-you cheat-I'll cheat' position. Altruistic punishers, on the other hand, will apply sanctions to those who behave unfairly, even if those same sanctions hurt themselves. In one of the experiments, a game, when the players are given the option of incurring a cost to themselves in order to punish free-riders and cheats, they regularly use the option of self-harming punishment. As a result, the rate of co-operation stays high and the group stays intact. This happens even though individual punishers, superficially at least, gain less from their action than it costs them. At a deeper and more evolutionary level, it may be that they are prepared to punish a cheat at a net loss to themselves, so that the group survives.

These experiments are relevant to the Toilet Program. When a matter is hard to drop, it could be that the 'altruistic punishers' will take the pain of the extra bureaucracy and delays in order that 'cheats do not prosper'. They may do this even if it would be better, in terms of efficiency and cost, for the organisation to allow the cheats to prosper. The Consultant would do well not to get too exasperated by this behaviour, which from the outside seems lunatic. Being on the 'outside' is the point: the Consultant is not actually in the group, and is therefore not part of its protective mechanism that has it that thwarting wrongdoers is more important than smooth running or efficiencies – 'we will continue to hurt ourselves and keep the group together rather than help ourselves and allow the occasional scoundrel to prosper'.

A social evolutionary understanding such as this can help a consultant work with a group's apparently redundant cross-checking protocols. The question becomes whether a consultant should, or can, move the mindset to a more efficiency-based one.

A final comment here: sometimes these matters are less to do with status quo bias or altruistic punishers than real effects in the real world that prevent change. The downside is too extreme and introducing the desired change is just too hard. It is like asking a diplomat to 'just crash through' a delicate negotiation. The experienced diplomat knows that this will not be construed as a leadership virtue of 'cutting through the noise' but a beginner's fault in not being able to read a multi-minefield situation and creating disasters that will take many years to patch up. Psychological and social explanations do have weight and explain many apparently self-punishing self-imposed restrictions, but other real-world factors also play their part, making it difficult to discern what solution is optimal, and how one can drop a burdensome item AND not compromise safety OR signal the end of protecting the integrity of the group.

Managing a Toilet program

So far our two examples – Alliance Stores and BioChem – have concerned very senior groups where all the authority needed to drop or modify a practice is present in the room. The program, however, can also successfully be used lower in the organisational hierarchy with teams and groups of teams, even though they may sometimes need to 'refer up' their recommendations for change. In this section you will find some advice on set-up, warm-up and process.

First of all, you can expect some nervous or excited laughter at the toilet image. Capitalise on this by retaining the toilet talk, so long as you don't go too far and offend people. They will be offended if they believe that you yourself are an immature character still stuck in potty phase of development. They need to know that you are attempting to channel their energy into a serious organisational task, and that the scatological imagery is only there to help the process. They need to know this, but you cannot say it – otherwise the metaphor loses its punch. So they have to pick it up as an unspoken contract between you and them. It goes something like this: 'It is an unusual way of going about business, but it definitely *is* business.'

When you have a large group comprising several teams, address the whole group, saying that you will break them into their local teams, and that you are going to ask them to do something quite difficult, but which at first seems a breeze. You are going to ask them to look at their own processes with a view to cutting out duplication, waste, unnecessary red tape, multiple rather than single point reporting, repeated but similar processes that are treated as one-offs every time, and the like. In the first instance they will be dealing within their own team, and later, for issues between their teams. (You can, of course, deal exclusively with wastage between teams – how they get in each other's way.) The Toilet Program is essentially a way of focusing on reduction. The chair and basket create a 'stage' and dropping the piece of paper becomes the drama, filled with interest and tension. People are transfixed by the piece of paper and its possible fate.

Encourage the belief that the participants actually do know where the waste is. They may have been too busy to look at it and find solutions, or perhaps there has never been the right forum to put their ideas forward. If the latter is the case, then today's their chance. Suggest to them that it is not for nothing that their manager has put on this day – he or she has as big a stake as they in getting rid of waste. Remind them that though the thought of dropping wasteful products or processes and 'flushing them away' is exciting, the process can sometimes be much tougher than they might have imagined.

Preparation

You saw in the case of Jim Phelps of Alliance Stores, that he did much of the preparation himself, and engaged whole teams of business analysts to help him. You also saw in the case of BioChem that the executives working in the Toilet Program took preparation most seriously and did extensive research beforehand. As well, it is sometimes the case that the consultant him or herself does the research, or some of it. Before the workshop begins, the consultant may engage with the senior manager on possible suggestions for matters that might be targeted. With the manager's backing, they might conduct a mini-survey in the organisation to ascertain the group's reputation with their customers. At all levels, a Toilet Program will work best when the participants have prepared beforehand for any necessary data, and to form their opinions on what they find.

Production

Produce a 'toilet' of some sort, and set it in the middle of the room. This can be a chair beside a wastepaper basket or small garbage bin. Set the chair next to the bin as illustrated. If the group or team leader seems too embarrassed at having something looking like a toilet, just have the bin on its own and rename the exercise as 'The Garbage' or whatever. We saw Jim Phelps manage a Toilet Program without any simulation of an actual toilet – he used a four-box matrix instead. As well as the whole process bringing the way the group operates into sharp focus (Clarity) to all participants, the toilet image and the paper held over it pushes up the existential moment (Vitality) for participants The point is, this is a process that focuses on one thing – elimination – and the image of a toilet or a garbage bin or, as we saw with Alliance, two boxes of a simple four-box matrix, is there to serve it.

If they have not had the chance beforehand to prepare for the day, get the groups to discuss what should be dropped and flushed away in their particular area. Ask them to write the matters down, one matter per page. You will have to judge the length of a sufficient time for discussion – somewhere between 30 to 60 minutes for junior groups seems about right. It is different for a senior team discussing company-wide practices that involve compliance, reporting, OH&S matters, etc. As we have seen with Alliance and BioChem, the preparation process might take much longer and involve roles such as the company legal officer, the head of Marketing or Accounting, Stores, Fleet, and so on. These persons may themselves need weeks of preparation beforehand.

On the day, a member comes out with his or her papers and sits on the chair beside the bin. They read the first item out for colleagues and hold it over the bin. Then the matter is either dropped into the bin, or not dropped. If the group in question and the immediate manager approves of the drop, but the level of sign-off for eliminating the item needs to be higher, she undertakes to advocate with the relevant senior person. If the item involves another group not in the room, someone can be deputed to go off line and

Figure 5.2 Chair and bucket representing toilet

clear it with that other group and to report back. This saves time, but be aware that such immediate access is not always possible on the day.

The process can arouse deep anxiety for the most senior managers in the room. They are vulnerable not only to discovery (in that they have allowed a longstanding practice that the group deems redundant), but to the fear of getting rid of something that has been part of the place for a long time (see the section on status quo bias above). They have to wear the risk factors of departing from the custom. 'What if a disaster happens that this very regulation or practice was meant to circumvent?' is the troubling question at the back of the manager's mind. As you can see, this tortured question fits with the idea of 'regret avoidance', also described above. The positive consequences of gains from action are awarded less weight than the pain of losses that might occur if one had done nothing.

Once the matters that are to be dropped have been dropped, the work of the group or its leader is to make referrals up to the level required. At Executive level this might sometimes be to the Board, but more often the Executive contains its own approval system. At levels lower than this, the matter might still be within the team's own remit, or may have to be worded and argued 'up the line'.

In commissioning a Toilet Program, the team and its leader have put time aside to hear the unique perspectives and concerns of their colleagues, and to seek new convergences and ways of being. Where a matter has not been able to be dropped, the Consultant might understand that organisations are systems in which people are continuously making meaning. They do so with special intensity in a Toilet program. The Consultant provides a forum where this meaning-making may change through the starkness of the toilet image itself, and the mild drama of having an item written on a piece of paper being dropped or not dropped. Further changes might be possible in the future, but for now the matter is closed.

References

Gintis, H., Bowles, S. Boyd, R. and Fehr, E. (2005). *Moral sentiments and material interests*. Cambridge, MA: MIT Press.

Kim, W. and Mauborgne, R. (2005). *Blue ocean strategy*. Boston, MA: Harvard Business School Press.

Chapter 6

The Dining Room
Align

Origins of the Dining Table process

When the words 'dining room' are said, one immediately sees a table, and it is indeed the table we will focus on in this Room. The business issues for the Dining Room involve *vision and alignment.*

The special technique for this Room is a process called 'Lay it on the Table'. This chapter will illustrate the technique, almost always through stories, and in multiple contexts.

The colloquial meaning of 'lay it on the table' is one of 'frank talk', and you will find plenty of that in the cases below. The process ticks all the boxes of Clarity, Vitality and Alignment, with special emphasis on the last – Alignment.

The first time I used Lay it on the Table I did not have a name for it. Actually, I was in a jam. The client group was 80 Catholic nuns, some of them quite elderly and on walking frames. Our working space – a large meeting room in an old convent – was extremely tight. It wasn't at all ideal for methods requiring physical movement. In that cramped room it was pretty hard to get around, which ruled out sociometric divisions, continua, 'voting with your feet' and other stock-in-trades of action methods.

Nuns are often associated with cuteness and caricature – naivety, wimples, veils, clanking rosary beads, gliding walks and so on. Well, not this group, and maybe not any other nuns, either. 'Cute' and 'naïve' just did not apply. These women were tough and had been in some of the worst trouble spots in the world, where primitive machismo ruled, and the fate of women was precarious. Domestic violence, rape, torture, malnutrition and child abuse was the daily experience of the people they looked after. Though their whole vocation began in the heavens, the life experience of these nuns ensured their feet were firmly on the ground.

Organisational alignment #1 'The Daisy and the Stone'

The sisters' issue was a vital one for them. It involved 'shared vision'. Shared vision is every CEO's dream: shared vision, or alignment, is a mental model of the future state of the organisation that provides a basis for action.

In this case, the issue was 'what is community?' The interpretation of 'community' affected every aspect of their lives – how they worked, how they lived, and with whom. The Constitution of their Order, some 400 years old, mandated living 'in community'. But the sisters in that meeting room had very different understandings of what 'living in community' meant. Some lived alone in run-down flats in the poor corners of the city; some lived in pairs or small groups in suburban houses, and some in traditional convents. Those who lived in flats or houses had no wish to return to the traditional convents in which they had spent the early part of their religious life. They wanted to continue living like 'normal' people – in a house or flat. Many of them lived the way they did because they were serious about being close to the most dispossessed of society, and wished to make their lives in the rundown housing of the very poor. Others were introverts, simply wanting a quiet space that was not shared with a dozen others. Others still liked traditional convents. Everyone had a preference and a view; all present were stakeholders in defending their vision of 'community'.

> The General of the order had travelled from Rome to sort things out (superiors of religious orders are often called 'Mother General' or 'the General'), and I had been invited to facilitate a two-day workshop with the whole Province to help the Sisters resolve several issues. 'Living in community' was only one of them. The early matters had gone well, but on Day 2 – the day of the 'community' issue – the conversations were vague and circular. We seemed to be getting nowhere.

In one of the breaks, I had the idea that these groups – the General and the Sisters, should 'lay it on the table' with each other, in the sense of being more frank with each other. The metaphor caught me: what if they could actually lay something on a table – a physical object that would represent their position or thoughts? The 'table', then, should be an actual table. 'Lay it on the Table' was born.

After the break I gave these instructions:

Each of you has ten minutes to find something in this room or immediately outside in the garden that represents 'community' for you. Bring the object back here, and I will suggest what to do next.

The nuns left the room and foraged around inside and outside the building. I suggested to the General that she should likewise find an object. She appeared startled, but agreed to do so.

When the ten minutes were up, the nuns were still struggling back into the room. They bore an extraordinary array of objects. The General had also arrived back with her object – a daisy. In the meantime, I had set up a table sideways to the audience, and a chair on each side so that at least the sides of the faces of the two speaking parties could be seen by all.

I invited the General to sit on one side of the table with her object, and say what it was and what it meant. Again she was startled, saying that she preferred 'to go last, when I have heard everyone'. I asked her to indulge me, saying that I recognised her preference, but that it was important that she go first. She bravely agreed. She sat out the front, and for the first time led with what she thought. She looked at the daisy, and then started to describe it – its commonness, its humbleness, the golden centre (which she said represented community) – and the petals on the outside of that centre, which she said were the individual nuns, each one separate, but always attached to the centre.

Having said her piece, the General was eager to leave the table. I asked her to stay. Lined up in front of it was a bunch of women, from 40 to 80 years old, holding the object that to them represented 'community'. Some had ferns; one had a cactus, another a stone, another a soft cushion, another a dry twig, another a glass of water and so on. I invited them to come up one by one and take the chair opposite the General, and put their object on the table.

Similarly to the process with the General, they were asked to describe their object. With the first couple of women to do this, the General was very affirming, saying in effect: 'That's very interesting, thank you' after they had said their piece. I began to intervene, saying,

Figure 6.1 Dining Room – table and chairs

> But Mother General, she has a stone, and you have a daisy. These are very different things. They don't seem to be compatible. You might need to argue why a daisy, or something like it, is what prevails in terms of community, or agree with her that the stone is the new way forward. What you are working on is vision, and it's difficult when vision is not aligned. I'm afraid this is the time to contest.

After a slow start, contest she did. She had to wrestle with each one of them, and she became easier with it, trying to understand their experience of community and their vision of it, at the same time as not giving up on the Constitution of the Order, which she was bound to uphold, or letting go her own vision of how 'community' should be enacted.

This is a difficult balance for any manager to keep – staying true to the vision (or changing it if they thought that their discussant had a better one), not overpowering their colleagues, and yet not giving up. In the case of the General, she also had to adjust her own quiet leadership style and deep respect for others and their opinions. She managed this, and all could see her integrity and goodwill as she did so.

Please note that it is important to instruct a Lay it on the Table group that the object, once laid, is to be left on the table. At the end of the process, an object from each person is on the table, and the group and the leader can see, as it were, the 'collective unconscious' arrayed: 'What have we here? What are we saying about ourselves?' Figure 6.2 shows the objects from an imaginary group of eight persons.

It will be clear by now that Lay it on the Table involves a projective technique: participants invest an apparently unrelated object – a daisy, a stone – with qualities and meanings of which the object is innocent. Projective techniques, such as the Rorschach test (not much now used in psychology, but highly used in market research), are said to tap into people's deep motivations, beliefs, attitudes and values in a way that may otherwise elude direct

Figure 6.2 Items on a table

questioning. To this degree, they are useful for getting at 'vision': What is really driving this leader? What is really driving these colleagues?

> The group was large. We did not get through all of the objects held by the participants in time. It seemed that the dozen or so objects that were on the table were a 'good enough' representation of participants' diverse ideas. We had other events on that final afternoon, and participants took the matter offline to work with another time. Members understood as never before what was in the General's mind about community when, given all the objects in the house and the grounds, she had reached out and selected the daisy. The General, for her part, was coming to know her own newly formed imagery, and that of the sisters.

The strangeness of translating a half-formed inchoate idea into a self-chosen object allows participants to express thought that originates on a different, perhaps deeper, level than might be tapped by writing down or talking about 'a vision'. This process is incredibly strong: to the best of my knowledge, the sisters never forgot that afternoon, and nor did I.

Organisational alignment #2: "The Cufflink"

Not long after my encounter with the nuns, I was engaged to run a two-day retreat for a large government financial agency – we'll call it the Government Finance Bureau (GFB). Present on the retreat were the senior executive and the next level of management below – about 35 people in all. The Lay it on the Table event took place outdoors in the extensive bushland grounds of the conference centre. I asked all participants, including the senior manager, Miles, to find an object that represented 'the GFB of the future – say, three years' time'.

Somewhat sceptical at this unusual request, participants wandered off into the roadsides and forest and each collected an object that gave them an idea of how the Bureau should be in the future. In the meantime, I arranged a table out the front, and the chairs in a shallow horseshoe two rows deep. As we were outside, the only table we could get was a rather rustic one, with bench seats.

Members brought back ferns and mossy things, green twigs, stones, pieces of timber, garden chairs and so on. As with the nuns, I asked Miles to go first. Unlike the Mother General, he was ready to launch straight away. He pulled a cufflink from his immaculate cuff, and laid it on the table. It was a tiny object, made even smaller by the context of being outdoors in the mountains. He held it up and rotated it slowly. The group leant forward to peer at it. I asked Miles to describe what he had placed on the table.

Miles: (Holding the cufflink aloft) This is the Bureau of the future. We'll be like this in three years' time.
Cons: What is it? What does it look like?
Miles: (Peering at the cufflink) It's a cufflink, it's round and it's small, with a dished bit in the middle.
Cons: Yes indeed, it's small. What else strikes you about it?
Miles: Well, except for the little dish, it's unornamented – pretty plain.
Cons: Pretty plain, eh?
Miles: You'll notice in the middle of the dish there's a little hole in the very centre.
Cons: Ah, so there is. What about the surface – could you describe that?
Miles: It's hard, quite hard.
Cons: Shiny?
Miles: No, it's a matt finish – a sheen, but not shiny.
Cons: What era does it belong to?
Miles: It's a Jensen you know – I'd call it 'timeless modern minimalist'.
Cons: I see. So the Bureau of the future is small.
Miles: Yes, small.
Cons: Hard.
Miles: Yes.
Cons: Dished.
Miles: Yes, like a funnel. Nearly all the money that comes to us goes straight through that hole in the centre to the Government. Very little gets stuck on the sides to pay for the Bureau.
Cons: Modern, minimalist and did you say 'timeless'?
Miles: I did. About a third of the client work we do now face-to-face will be done online, and our website will relentlessly direct people away from the call centre to forms that they can download and submit electronically.

Cons: Oh, I see. And with a sheen, but not shiny.
Miles: Yes, we won't be in the glamorous shiny building that we're now in. Since most of our work is back-office, we may not even be in the city. We're becoming a no frills group.
Cons: And the sheen?
Miles: The sheen is good practice. We do our work well, and we do it quickly. The sheen helps reduce friction. Little stays on the surface, that is, stays with us, and practically all the run-off goes straight to the Government. That's our job.

The Consultant's role in these interviews is that of Naïve Inquirer who leads clients into a deeper description of the object – they talk more and more 'through' it. The image leads to the words. Few people have much of an idea, when they choose a twig, say, that they will end up talking at length about the twig and therefore the company's twigginess. Again, Lay it on the Table is a projective technique – the explanation of the choice is the justification for choosing it, and comes afterwards. Miles may well have chosen his cufflink for deep reasons already articulated in his mind, or because it allowed him to stay seated in his place – we don't know. But my experience is that the words follow the object choice, rather than that one has the words and at last finds a suitable vehicle for them. The object leads and inspires the thoughts. It helps people access 'the words to say it'.

There are advantages and disadvantages to every type of boss for an employee, and for that matter, every type of sponsor when you are a consultant. Miles had started out rather enigmatically, and the first minutes were a little fraught. It had been a line ball whether he would participate at all. Had he not agreed, the exercise could not have gone ahead – it is pointless to manufacture a vision experience into which the Chief Visionary will not enter. Fortunately, Miles relaxed enough to allow the Consultant to do the exercise, and once warmed up, he was a meticulously observant participant who may well have gone further than he'd imagined when he so casually chose his object.

The set-up and instructions for Lay it on the Table are relatively simple. The art of running the process is more difficult: it requires the consultant to 'milk' the image so that participants project their innermost visions on an object that they may originally have chosen quite casually. You have to milk it hard, but avoid being corny or exasperating to clients by badgering them.

> When it came to participants bringing their object to the table, Miles was more than ready to dispute the vision they had with the one he had. You can imagine that there is a great deal of difference between a tree fern and a cufflink when used as an image for work. Miles engaged with each member of his management team as they came up with their

> object. They questioned his cufflink, he questioned their tree fern, plant, twig or other object. He had a 'dry' view of work – it could only provide certain satisfactions and could not and should not take the place of family and friends. Many of his staff had 'wet' views – work was a social structure that should serve business outcomes but also many other social and individual purposes.

The managers were given a deep insight into the mind of their boss. That insight had come via his symbolic representation, even if he initially may not have put a great deal of thought into what he chose. When asked to describe his object and to speak 'through' it, he was not working on a 'spin', but manifesting his inner, and for want of a better word, 'unconscious' vision. His version of the organisation on that day was certainly news to his managers. It was also utterly memorable to them; in their careers they were survivors and forgetters of countless dot point presentations and endless vision statements. But not this one.

By way of postscript, within three years the Bureau had relocated to a regional city, conducted most of its business online, and shed a third of its workforce. The cufflink prevailed absolutely.

Contrast in time – past and present: Aeon's decline

Our next example comes from a very different industry – manufacturers and suppliers of DIY home products. The process involves **two** objects per person, and in this (rather rare) case, using the manager himself as the facilitator.

> Aeon Tools manufactures and imports handyman products. Mitch has been its General Manager for about six months, making his debut in the business pages as one of the boy wonders of manufacturing. A large man of 29, stylishly dressed and with a background in marketing, he is young in a trade that favours age and experience. He wears shiny black riding boots, deep blue shirts open at the neck, and smooth Italian-looking jackets. He is funny, buoyant, self confident and intensely focused. This focus can come at you suddenly, unseating you when you have a moment earlier been laughing at one of his jokes, or making one of your own.
>
> The parent company is hoping that Mitch's drive and ambition will work for Aeon's rather traditional and highly unionised manufacturing culture.
>
> Though Aeon was still market leader in the region, its sales had been declining. Mitch himself had been at Aeon when this decline had taken place, but had not been General Manager at that stage. He tells me that he wants to see how his Exec views the company, and that he wants a 'read-out' on how things have been going since he took over.

Lay it on the Table with two objects is ideal for such a brief. The then/now format automatically builds in contrast, which immeasurably invokes our consulting values of Clarity, Vitality and Alignment. It enrols participants in developing their own picture of how the organisation 'was then' and 'is now'. This picture, stronger than words, allows the manager to see the archetypes that each participant reveals: What is their unconscious image of the organisation? What are the words to use when they are staring at an object they have chosen, and conventional management-speak just doesn't fit?

Unlike the nun's daisy, or Miles's cufflink, where at the outset a resolution is sought ('Make my way our way'), the aim here is to foster generativity and develop new possibilities. This might mean altering conventional narratives that limit new thinking. One way to do this is to go out of language into form (Miles, initially flippantly, chooses a cufflink) and then from form back into more richly elaborated language – (Miles is encouraged to describe the features of the cufflink at length – size, shine, hardness and so on).

In the example below, Mitch had been coached to facilitate the Lay it on the Table session himself. In our steady consulting relationship, it was evident that Mitch had the psychological acuity to do the job. Provided one has a manager capable of it (a good sense of timing, knowing how to get the other to talk 'through' an object, etc.), this can be preferable to the Consultant asking the questions. The manager knows what is relevant. Do not attempt it, however, if you think the manager will not be up to the task. This leads to a horribly bungled session, and loss of face to the manager. If the manager loses face, it will be deemed your fault, and it probably is.

> I set up the room horseshoe-style with the table out the front, and gave the initial instructions: 'Go outside and find two objects – one to depict the old Aeon and one that represents the Aeon now. Take no more than ten minutes for your search, and be ready to start back on time.'
>
> Members went out of the room to select their objects, and then individually laid them on the table in front of Mitch. Some examples of what they laid and what questions the manager asked them follow. They are reported fairly fully so that you can get the sense of the exercise. Please attend to Mitch and the ways he gets participants to talk 'through' their object.
>
> Alex chose a piece of driftwood (snatched from an artistic array in the hotel foyer), and a watermelon seed from the fruit platter at lunch. He said the old Aeon was like that old piece of driftwood, drifting along passively, being attacked by the elements. The new Aeon, on the other hand, was like a seed – something living that has to interact with the environment – with water, with soil, with air, with temperature – to survive. The new Aeon was a place where he could look forward to going to work every day, a place with a master plan that he could attach to,

one to which he had made a contribution. Such a plan, said Alex, would have a sales strategy, a marketing strategy and an operational strategy that all fitted together.

Mitch: (realising that Alex has rapidly switched from describing the object to talking in conventional management terms) How do we focus on the seed?
Alex: By thinking of the watermelon at the end. The vision. But also the process – the air, the water, the environment – in other words our sales strategy, our marketing strategy, our operational strategy.
Mitch: (cutting across) What is the air? (Alex and Mitch talk for some time about air and water and environment)
Alex: We have to think of the new thing that we will become.
Mitch: That's fascinating, because you're talking about us as young again, rather than old. Yet we're an old company. This has changed my own thinking a lot. Are we really driftwood? Our profits are good.
Alex: They are good, but they are completely steady, inert, in other words.
Mitch: How do we become young, like a start-up, like a seed?

They continue in this vein for a while, with Mitch pushing the driftwood and seed metaphor as hard as he can without straining it. What Alex says is far more original and compelling when Mitch can get him to stay with the driftwood or the seed, and not to lapse into conventional business talk. Alex says that he wouldn't mind being driftwood, taken where the market goes, so long as they had a sail and a rudder. Mitch urges him to tell where they would be going if they had a rudder, and how could something be at the same time a rudderless driftwood and a ruddered driftwood, given there were advantages to floating where the market went, and disadvantages to that. They continue talking in this manner for some time.

Bev chose the table itself ('functional, solid, but not going anywhere') and a set of forks (borrowed from the hotel dining table) with pointy tines, most of which were aligned in the same direction. The forks symbolised that Aeon had 'lots of things on the go, but some of them were sharp, and could hurt'.

Mitch: How do you get from a table to a fork?
Bev: You don't. A table is good, but it's got be able to go places. (pauses) Perhaps by getting rid of some forks – maybe lots of them.
Mitch: What are some of the dangers?
Bev: Focus on short-term profits, e.g. acquisitions. People are on the threshold; they could tip either way. They need some wins on the

Chapter 6: The Dining Room   63

	board; they need to feel good about themselves. There should be a top five priorities, but we have 41. No one can concentrate.
Mitch:	(Noticing that he had inadvertently led Bev away from the image, attempts to return to it.) So we've got too many forks, have we? If we had to ration our forks, how would we know which ones to throw out?
Bev:	All of them add value. And most of our forks are in the same direction, which is much better than before. But we have too many of them. We're short on people. We have to deliver a pretty big stretch at the best of times, but now we're short, so it's even harder.
Mitch:	So, all the things we have to get rid of are good in themselves.
Bev:	Yes, that's what makes it hard. Getting rid of obviously bad things is easy.
Mitch:	I'm not so sure about that – the easy part, I mean. Tell me three bad forks that I should push off this table.
Bev:	Oh, ah (embarrassed) These three.
Mitch:	Push them off. Go on!
Bev:	(Wincing) OK, here we go. (Pushes them off. They make a big clatter as they fall.)
Mitch:	Can you name these three?

> Even though the group is startled, Mitch, so far as he can, keeps exploring the metaphor rather than permitting use of the conventional business dialect with which they are all familiar.

After all participants have presented their individual objects, it is helpful to have a team debrief. The Consultant can lead this with questions such as, 'What are you making of your collective images?' Consultants can also take an Appreciative Inquiry tack, and ask questions that move the group into the future. Make the 'there' into 'here' by using your interviewing skills; role reverse each participant into 'myself-in-the-future'.

Note that Mitch did not place his own objects on the table for the Aeon of past and present. He was concerned that it could have been perceived as 'grandstanding' of him to plug the present, under his leadership, and unfavourably contrast it with the past, under his old boss. The second reason went beyond protocol: Mitch wanted to generate new possibilities, rather than to solve problems. He was more interested in discerning the weight and direction of the prevailing narratives than he was to arrive at to a particular point of reform, as Mother General had, or reveal a vision of the way the organisation was to become, as Miles had done with his cufflink. Just as he had hosted the Lay it on the Table process, Mitch also ran the debrief with his managers. He was perfectly capable of harvesting the ideas in which he was most interested, and the directions in which he wished to nudge the company forward. He was quite easy with the idea that that organisational realities are maintained and indeed created in many 'conversations', and that he had just run a spectacularly rich and symbolic visual conversation where different 'realities' were created by each person who came out. Each of his managers, as did Mitch himself, had their own sense of the organisation, and also had to make sense of the meanings of others.

Lay it on the Table with Aeon was a highly successful event that enhanced relationships and communications, and allowed Clarity, Vitality and Alignment more room in the company. People did settle into a new vision of the future, and the stories around it, co-created with Mitch.

Contrast in time – present and future

Vision statements are meant to raise people's sights and lead them on. They can also make people groan and put their heads in their hands. Their easily parodied slogans, can, with minimal editing, be substituted for one another. They are replete with recycled words and phrases like 'we will improve the quality of life for our customers', 'we will set the standards for value and quality', 'we will be the employer of choice' and 'we will be the leader in our markets'. They are hardly ever concrete, or indeed, a picture. They're always words, no matter the close the connection of 'vision' is to 'sight'. You are being asked to see it, but are not shown it.

A Lay it on the Table 'vision' is one that can mobilise people by feel, sight and hearing to enter into the future. Its dense descriptions allow them readily to see the future in action, the transitions they have to make, and their individual imagined selves as part of it. Its imagery is naturally stark and dynamic, and the narrative rich and colourful, or, as we saw with 'The Cufflink' (equally a 'vision'), minimal and realistic. Lay it on the Table for Vision needs a 'thick' narrative description of events, actions, and experiences. Participants see the picture, handle the picture, and put themselves in the picture by describing what's around them, and how they got there. They create the picture, and argue or agree with the pictures of colleagues and even their boss, just as we saw in 'The Daisy and the Stone'.

You have seen the basic technique of using two objects for Lay it on the Table in the DIY case above. There, the two objects represented the past and the present. You have also seen cases where the objects represent the future – 'daisy' and 'cufflink'. As it is a relatively easy transition to imagine a use for two objects to represent the present and the future, I will not indicate the procedures by means of a case, but simply set out some ideas, recipe-style, that might be useful.

1. Only use the manager as facilitator if you are utterly confident that they will bring it off. This is a difficult task, and Mitch's talent is rare.
2. Talk 'through' the objects as far as possible, getting ever thicker descriptions.

Chapter 6: The Dining Room

3. 'How you are going to make it' is more dynamic than the passive 'how you would like it to be' for the second object.
4. Remember from other examples of Lay it on the Table, that the objects are physical and actually laid on the table. They are kept there till the session ends. Though they serve a metaphorical purpose, they are not thought bubbles or fanciful descriptions, but things.
5. The path to creativity in this process lies in setting aside customary language (therefore thinking) and modes of operation (overheads, discussion) and taking on a more visual and metaphorical language. You want associations, and new ways of seeing things.
6. The key to the Now-and-the-Future process is to fully expand the description of each object, and then to link them. One of the biggest questions in a two-object Lay it on the Table is 'How do you get from one state to the other?

What is our life like now we have arrived here?
What are our customers' lives like now we have got here?
How long did it take us get here?
Who did what to get here?
Who did not want us to get here (e.g. competitors, members of our own staff who feared change, etc.)?
What did we do to ameliorate the risks of them stopping us?

Stay with the image. If you make immediate reference back to the company, you will snip too early the buds of new thinking thrust up by the image, and cut back the rich associations that lie inside. Allow the metaphor to flower as far as possible go before returning to the referent. This takes skill and courage.

After you have exhausted the possibilities of the metaphor, begin the workaround, returning to direct talk about the company.

In 12 months' time, is A (first object) still around, or has it completely gone?
Who in this company most likes A?
A and B (second object) are two very different entities. Seems to me they have nothing in common. How can one of them transition to the other when they are so unlike each other?

How will you prevent B from reverting back to A?

Only at the end might one ask a question directly about the company, for example 'In terms of setting the vision, what are you actually saying that's different?'

A visual and tactile process allows the co-designers of a company's future to look at problems more quickly than if they were described in words alone. Through the description of the experiences of employees and customers, it becomes clearer what one must do to reach the desired future state. These 'visions' are effective because they not only describe the attributes of the desired destination but also elaborate on what life will be like when it is reached. The use of present tense in Lay it on the Table descriptions strengthens the process: the future must be possible because it is 'already' happening. These thick descriptions provide for a distinctive comparison between the 'here' and the 'there' by relating it to the real experience of those likely to be part of it. Understanding, strong and analytic, comes through a visceral experience of 'being there'.

Note: There are other uses for the Dining Room apart from Lay it on the Table. The Dining Room is an excellent Room for the Innovation Hub, as we saw earlier, and colleagues and I have used it there many times for innovations concerning customer service, alliances, partners and suppliers.

Chapter 7

The Balcony
See

A systemic view – Gale Force

Claxton Brothers, a large printing and box-manufacturing firm, had been started by the two brothers in the 1950s. In the last ten years, long after the brothers' deaths, Claxton's had progressively fallen on hard times, strangling itself in a web of its own controls, and slowly losing its customer base.

After failed attempts by external consultants, and furious debate within Senior Exec, the CEO decided to get 'The Force'. He made head of Marketing, Gale Palmer, EO of business improvement, reporting directly to him. Gale shot from the hip and earned her nickname 'Gale Force' or more simply 'The Force'. A woman of disconcerting charisma, she was not popular in high quarters because of her ungrammatical writing, the speed (they would say 'haste') of her decision-making, and her loud jewellery. Others thrilled to her likeable vulgarity and canny instinct for where her industry was heading. She guarded her division like a vixen her lair, and was a tough-minded enemy of groupthink. She inspired, coaxed, cajoled, scolded, pleaded and did anything needed to get her team to meet its deadlines. They did meet them, and they did adore her.

Gale soon found that managing change throughout the whole of Claxton's was very different from managing change in Marketing at Claxton's.

I was doing what they (senior management) wanted me to do, but at the same time they didn't want it. They wanted the result, but to close their eyes on the reality – that people would have to change, that people would have to go. They wanted me to shake the place up, but without the shaking, if you know what I mean.

Heifetz and Linsky's use of the Balcony metaphor – 'getting off the dance floor and going to the balcony' has now become part of the business lexicon. Being 'on the balcony' means stepping away from the middle of action ('the dance floor') and asking: 'What's really going on?'

On a dance floor, the dancers are swept up in the music, the excitement, the action. They are conscious of their own dancing prowess, their partner and the people they bump into, sometimes literally. If they were asked, 'How was the dance?' they may reply that the music was terrific, that their partner is an excellent dancer and that it was great to 'just let go and float with the rhythm'. If, on the other hand, they were standing on a balcony overlooking the dance floor, and were asked, 'How was the dance?' they might reply that the men tended to congregate together; that a tight knit group of couples never moved from their little circle; that more people got up to dance when the music was 60s style, and so on. That kind of perspective is typical of a balcony view.

On most days your clients are swept up in the action, immersed in power plays, and skewered by compliance, reports, meetings, performance reviews, interviews and deadlines. In all this organisational noise, it's hard to detect patterns, or divine the underlying forces that make things what they are. Leaders think of themselves influencing the organisation, but less often of how the organisation is influencing them.

That is why Consultants need a 'place' to take their clients away, out of the system in which they are embroiled so that they can look at it and their part in its continuance.

That place is the Balcony

Understanding 'what's going on' requires observing from a height and a distance. Only when the system is understood (a tall order), can one usefully skip back down to the dance floor to make things happen. Ideally, a leader is in both places at once, like a good athlete, able to play the game and observe it at the same time. But that's a rare gift, and the product of hard experience. It will do, for the moment, to prise your client from the dance floor and make your way upstairs together. Seeing systems means seeing the landscape 'out there' and how that landscape interacts with the person next to you – your client. Even the most technical of problems in business seem to have accompanying personal, relationship and management issues that affect how, or whether, the technical problems get resolved.

When working with a client on the Balcony, it is tempting to locate what is wrong and who is wrong. But then we will only be seeing part of the system – the part to which the *others* are contributing. When the client is on the Balcony looking at a problem, it needs to be brought home that he or she – the person right there next to you leaning over the railing – is part of that problem. Doing this is not to extend the blame game: this 'part' may not be 50 per cent or even 5 per cent, but part nonetheless. At the very least, they are allowing others to act in a way that sustains the problem.

As a 'Room' in Our House, the Balcony is designed for your clients to see their own organisation as a system. A 'system' is a set of interacting components, each part influencing the other parts to make up a complex whole. That implies constant ripple effects – change in one part means change in the whole. A systems view helps to locate root causes and the ways a problem is being maintained. Taking such a view helps leaders move towards understanding and solutions that last. With the height and distance afforded by the Balcony, they can appreciate the socially and contextually intertwined nature of organisational life.

In providing the following depiction of the work with Gale, I would like to stress that her situation is only one of many for which Balcony work is suitable. The Balcony is designed to promote a very broad view where clients see patterns and assign meaning to them. Gale had a particular issue with finding influencers who could help her, but there are many other uses of the Balcony. Here is a short list. Try to get the client to work visually in each case, using the magnetic figures.

- *Show the fault lines in this organisation. Also depict the conditions that have given rise to them. How may your client be playing a part, albeit unwittingly, in their continued existence?*

- *Where are the green shoots - the niches of innovation - and how are these sustained or thwarted? Who is already trying to make change happen, and how may your client help them?*
- *Looking at this organisation as a whole, what would be an immersive scenario of the future that engages people at an emotional and intellectual level? Use the height and distance of the Balcony to "connect the dots" and create a big story of change.*
- *What are other companies in the same field doing, with special focus on outliers and fast movers? Show these, and how and where they impact your client's organisation.*
- *Name three possible future market conditons created by major economic or demographic changes that will affect your client's organisation.*

To see some of the techniques that a consultant may use on the Balcony, let us return to the case of Gale, who, having enjoyed great success as head of Marketing at Claxton's, is trying to influence her whole organisation on an adaptive problem.

> For all her earthiness, Gale was an idealist. She was highly attuned to people's relationships with her personally, but less aware of their relationships with each other, or how these connections affected outcomes. Over the years, she had handpicked most of the Marketing staff herself, and their viability in the company largely depended on their relationship with her. She had little sense that organisations were human networks that seldom ran on the purity of an idea, and that other factors – mostly sociometric – shaped their vote.

Duan et al. (2014) have written about a technique called 'snowball sampling' to find and use the power of 'hidden influencers' – those networks of influence that operate below the radar. Informal influencers exist in every organization, across industries, cultures and geographies, the authors argue. They are the people other employees look to for input, advice, or ideas about what's really happening in a company. They therefore have a large influence on what employees believe about the future, and their willingness to support or resist change.

Influencer patterns almost never follow the organisational chart, and are not easily predicted by role, such as being managers and senior managers. Gale could snowball sample by constructing a simple, anonymous e-mail survey to ask, for example: *'Who do you go to when you want to know what's really happening here?'* or *'Whose advice do you trust?'* By asking employees to nominate three to five people she could quickly identify a revealing set of influencers at Claxton's. When the names of nominees start to be repeated – often, after only three to four rounds – she can be confident she has got them.

Gale was not ready for this yet. She thought it 'shabby', for example, that decisions taken at a meeting depended on loyalties within the various networks – who owed a favour to whom, who had a grudge against whom, who was standing in the way of whom. Her natural instinct was to build passionately on the ideal, the reform itself. Within Marketing at Claxton's, that had worked. In the wider Claxton's, it didn't.

Conrad's chief problem was to find ways of harnessing the singular style that had made Gale so effective in her own division, yet was failing as she persisted with her old solutions. Claxton's needed her fire, yet loathed it. Conrad had to manage a way of allowing her to keep her ethical views intact, yet temper her contempt for any form of organisational politics, negotiation or compromise. Gale was at once naïve and a visionary – Conrad had to educate the former quality without losing the latter.

Where to look? Loyalties, tuning and bandwidth

Heifetz and his colleagues (2009) suggest three useful places to look at from the Balcony when one wants to see how the system is influencing the person: Loyalties, Tuning and Bandwidth. I have transformed some of their insights to a visual and active approach suitable for Our House.

When using visual representation, start the client with simple magnet-backed shapes – circles, triangles, squares, etc., and then, if the case requires it, with recognisable figures of various sorts. The reasons for this choice will become clearer as we examine several cases involving setting out a system with moveable objects. Still using Gale's reform agenda as our case study, let us see how Conrad could work with 'Loyalties' within Gale's system.

Loyalties

To introduce magnets to nervous organisational clients, it often pays to start them with an organisational chart format. A chart comforts people who might otherwise feel diffident about using magnets ('too precious, too psychological'). A chart is reassuringly no-nonsense, and not too distant from overheads of their organisation they have seen dozens of times before.

The first step is to ease the client into the visual mode. Using round black magnets, Conrad asks Gale to set out the Claxton organisational chart up to level 3.

The next step is to identify people who already share the client's view of the reform process, and for the client to replace the black counters representing those people with another colour, say green, or another shape,

72 Our House: Visual and Active Consulting

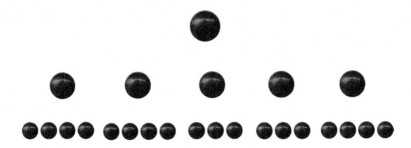

Figure 7.1 Gale's organisational chart

e.g. a triangle. (For the purposes of this illustration, printed here in black and white, we are using shapes rather than colours.)

Next, are people who were opposed to the client's ideas, or opposed to the client him or herself. Replace the black counters with a different colour, say red, or shape, e.g. squares, for these people. We are using squares here.

And last, are the neutrals or 'don't knows'. Replace the remaining black counters with one further colour, say white, or shape – circles – for these people.

After this three-part process, Gale's chart looked like this – the six magnets connected by the dotted line in the lower part of the diagram show the location of the next piece of work, to be elaborated:

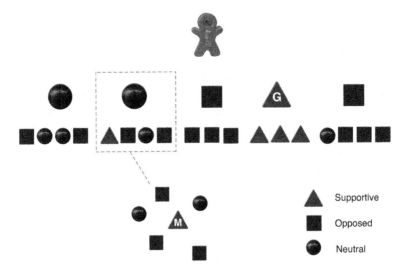

Figure 7.2 Gale's elaborated magnets

By placing herself in the picture, Gale has taken what psychologists (e.g. Grossmann et al. 2014) call a 'self-transcendent' viewpoint. That is, she is making the picture, but she is also *in* the picture. She sees herself as a triangle, occupying a position, just like anyone else on the board. This simple act of self-distancing (being observer and observed at the same time) has a function more capable of transformation than a simple friends-and-enemies mapping, or a 'getting the numbers' political exercise. It involves taking into account others' perspectives: they are actors in a situation just as she is. It's the beginning of leadership – playing the game and observing the game at the same time.

> Gail finds that she can be champion of her cause, and also the distanced observer of a network of relationships. On the Balcony, she can observe how things work.
>
> She can also see how isolated she is – the only triangle at her level, and having only one triangle on the level below her. She 'kind of' knew that before, but now it is arrayed visually. Little wonder that she is feeling isolated. She also begins to note that her loyal triangles in her own former team of Marketing are affecting her as much as she them. If she were to form a strong alliance with a square or a circle, would that be seen by them as a 'betrayal of lineage', or a 'selling out' of some sort? Are they hemming her in, 'forcing' her not to change, banging her own loyalty drum too hard in her ear for her to think straight?

Whether or not the 'betrayal' theme is valid, you may see already the many consulting points that emerge from such a tableau, despite its form being 'only' a conventional org chart. My mission in this book is not to advertise massive interventions from powerful and arcane consulting tools; rather, it is to show how small and humble interventions, such as providing a 'stage' of some sort, or the use of simple magnetic figures that can be bought from office supplies, can provide very strong consulting points for your client. Look at Lay it on the Table, for example – enormous output of vision and grounds for alignment from the simplest of mechanisms – a table, two chairs, some found objects, a dialogue. Look at the Basement: draw a pillar on a sheet of A3 and have people come and stand under it, so they have to look up at the pillar and the imaginary house it is holding up. Ask them if that pillar is strong enough for the job. The stage element, slight though it be, raises the stakes, somehow, and helps clients think about their business. They get clear, they are alive, and they are engaged.

Back to the magnets. Using this method, clients, in this case Gale, now have the whole top three levels of the organisation coded in terms of their response to a proposal. A helpful place to start work is with the triangles:

inquire what the client is doing to maintain 'triangle' loyalty, and whether that loyalty is helping or impeding her. Loyalty can be investigated from every angle. You might point out the risk of taking triangles' loyalty for granted, since each triangle may well be loyal to the client, but have other affiliations with other projects and bosses and friends to honour as well. Each of their own individual networks is likely to contain some neutrals (Circles) towards the reform, and perhaps some hostile Squares. This is true for every counter on the board, each of them the centre of their own universe a little node wired up in all directions to other little nodes, many of which are not even in the picture. But they might well live in the land of the 'hidden influencers'.

'How is this different to a stakeholder analysis?' The difference is essentially that this lens is a sociometric one – that is, it focuses on relationships *between* all the parties, as well as directly on the proposal. Stakeholder analyses tend to focus on the relationship of the stakeholders to a central event or proposal – a very helpful spokes-and-hub view, by the way. But organisational politics is not only, or indeed may rarely be, a 'pure' reaction to an idea – a golden line, as it were, from the rim to the hub. It's messier than that, and not so golden.

This process allows the consultant to drill down to an individual triangle. Please examine the cluster second from the left, involving the Triangle whose boss was a Circle, and whose colleagues were Squares or Circles. What pulls of loyalty or coercion might be on that lone Triangle in the cluster to having a conversion experience and becoming a Circle or a Square? You can make a little side-show on the board with Triangle as the centre – an elaboration of Triangle's alliances and loyalties – his own web of connection.

> Gale placed some other triangles next to her original Triangle (Triangle M), and added some Circles and Squares. Conrad and Gale then discussed Triangle's political situation and how Gale might support Triangle M to keep supporting her.

They could then inquire about each Triangle, Circle and Square selected as being close to Triangle M, and what those tugs of loyalty might mean for Triangle's attachment to the reform program. This process exploits the magnets' ability to be moved, and to depict attachment or loyalty visually by means of showing each player's nearness or far-ness, both to Triangle M and each other. The Consultant can discuss the possibility of gaining the allies of the allies, or conversely of losing a prime ally – Triangle M – back to one of their other allegiances in their networks. The client begins to see the possibility of working within sub-groups on the change agenda.

This exercise involves the client developing leadership skills by a better understanding of the forces at play within an organisational system, and

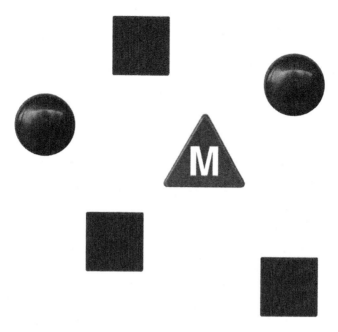

Figure 7.3 Detail of the cluster around Triangle M

how the leader must engage those forces to make headway with a reform agenda. It is not merely a matter of 'getting the numbers' in organisational politics. One is reluctant openly to vote for an issue when the person to whom you owe favours is voting against it. Through moving the little counters, the client comes to see each person on the board as always at the centre of a sliding set of relationships, favours, loyalties, affinities and paybacks. Many of these relationships have long and shifting histories – the client's project is but one factor in them. Neither Gale nor her project is the centre of people's lives. Indeed, in her campaign she might lose an ally or gain one, and the loss or gain might have nothing to do with her or her project.

> When deeply internalised, this systemic view can lead to humility and the beginnings of wisdom. Gale cannot push this reform through by force of her personality, as she so often had done in Marketing. The event that she cares about so passionately and that is so central in all her thinking is but one of many events in her colleagues' lives. Like any rational person, she knows this; but it didn't *feel* true until she could spend some time moving the counters representing Triangle's sociometric positioning. She comes to recognise the limits of her knowledge – she knows fiercely what is driving her, but she has little idea of what is driving others, even when those 'others' are close allies.

> As well as the glum possibility of Gale actually losing an ally (Triangle M) and his crossing over to become a neutral or hostile colleague, there is the possibility of M persuading one of his colleagues – a Circle, in our example – to come onside with the change program and become a Triangle. 'Conversion' can work either way. But how to help that happen becomes part of Conrad's process with Gale. She can work through M, or she can work directly with that circle, trying to understand Circle's networks and pressures, and present to Circle her understanding of where Claxton's should be headed. She can work in this way with any figure on the board.
>
> The Circles can be just as dangerous as the Squares: they are the most numerous group and their own agenda is often hard to ascertain. Their opposition could be as simple as resentment at their customary way of doing things being disrupted. Their support for the status quo and apathy about change may come less from idealism, and more from the fact that the status quo is familiar territory. They have worked out their ways of being in that territory and are comfortable there. Conrad advises Gale never to forget that Circles' amorphous dislike of *any* change may morph into active resistance and determination to push the change agent out altogether. Bad handling can rapidly turn people's mild disaffection with a change program into a buzzing cloud of outrage. Though the Circles' opposition at any moment may be low key, it can rapidly switch them into an angry swarm, bent on fatally stinging the invader.

Reader, perhaps you can already see many other coaching posts along the way for dealing with Circles and Squares. Let us not dwell there just now. The point here is to illustrate some uses of the Balcony that can give clients a solid platform, away from the hubbub of the dance floor, on which to map and plan the change process, whatever your favourite change theory is. That platform allows them to witness the structural and social ramifications of something new being introduced into a system. Having witnessed it on the board, they are in a better position of knowing what to do next in the hurly burley of the dance floor when they return. As they do more work with the magnets, clients increase their ability to appraise complex social events in ways that promote insight and closure. They have clearer and more coherent understanding of the system they are trying to change.

> Gale is nervous about being, as she says, 'manipulative' in using any other stance than a direct and passion-fuelled call to arms. It was important for her to come to terms with the new approach and to see that it was not shady or against principled practice. She was beginning to understand the 'opposition' and its networks, seeing each person as their own centre of the pulls of loyalty and the pushes of power, 'just

like I am, I suppose' as she said to Conrad. With the knowledge of conflicted loyalties and webs of obligations, she could ethically explain over a lunch or cup of coffee to the person she was attempting to influence just what she was seeking and why, and not see this practice as grubby or hypocritical. In a series of coffees and drop-in chats, she was effectively making a one-to-one business case with each of her Circles and Squares. She was but doing them the courtesy of at last acknowledging that to them her reforms were only obviously good to herself, and that the proposed changes might well interrupt the relationships that they already had. She was able to drop her 'to the barricades' approach as the only one possible.

Still working sociometrically, she and Conrad developed a plan to involve formal and informal leaders in all phases of her proposed cultural changes. She wanted them to become models of the new ways of acting, and stay with it through the pain. But first of all she had to understand that pain, and talk with them about their losses. We know from the pioneering work of Nobel Laureate Daniel Kahneman (2011) that fear of loss is a much stronger motivator than anticipation of gain. Kahneman also established that the pain of loss is greater than the pleasure of gain. Gale could explore with others – triangles, circles and squares – the consequences for them if her change program were successful: what would they have to lose personally, and what the effect in their networks of the new reforms would be.

Adding an action component – role reversal

In the case study with Gale you have already seen that the Balcony is the spot to take some deep breaths and look at the whole. It gives your clients the distance to view their opposition's stances and see them at least as genuinely held positions, 'wrong' though they might be. We focused on Loyalties and looked at the sociometry – essentially peoples' networks around a given criterion – that allows a leader to understand some of the social restraints on change.

This next section will focus more on the content of people's issues, allowing the leader to reflect deeply on the pro and contra points of different positions if they are to lead adaptive change. Let's go back to Gale.

> Gale's sense of being Truth's Missionary had blinded her to the value of different perspectives. Managing people's sensitivities was new to her – she was more used to charismatic conversions. Conrad asked Gale to think of her four staunchest opponents and, now using figurative counters, place them on the board. She could do so in a hierarchy of opposition, if she liked.

Figure 7.4 Gale's top opponents

These people represent some of the major constraints Gale is to face if she wants to make things happen. Conrad asked her to stand by the whiteboard and, holding the first counter in her hand, 'become' that person – let's say her name was Jane. To warm her up, Conrad interviewed Gale in role (see The Attic for a description of the interview-in-role process) as 'Jane', briefly asking about her background, where her office was, how long she had been at Claxton's, and so on. Conrad then asked her – still in role as 'Jane' – what her views were on Gale's proposed changes at Claxton's; what they meant for her people; what they meant for her colleagues, and what they meant for Claxton's traditions – 'the way we do things around here'. Gale slipped into role easily as 'Jane', and spoke sincerely, setting out why she opposed the changes, and what she thought of Gale's competence, sincerity etc., for initiating them.

Repeat the process with the other major opponents, in each case asking the client to take a counter off the board, hold it, stand in a different position from where they had stood as 'Jane' (a tiny bit of theatre – just taking a step – helps the warm-up to 'I am now a different person') and 'become' person #2 – Luciana, not Gale's favourite person, as you can see from the figure chosen. Follow the same process with persons #3 and 4, in Gale's case, the top hat man, and the owl – your own client, should you work in this way – will of course have different figures. Understandably, there will be much commonality in the positions of the selected people, but also some significant differences. Take notes of what the client says in role as each person.

When the client has set all the counters back on the board, sit them down and from your notes relay what they had said in role about their proposed changes.

Gale was calm during this process; she had moderated her righteousness about the 'absurd' opposition. By having 'become' one of them and speaking about the company from their viewpoint, she could recognise at least the sincerity of the various opposing positions. This further took the fanatical heat out of her own position, and added, inter alia, an interest in going back to talk with her colleagues: she could find out if she got it right when she role-reversed.

Even though Gale retained a firm determination about the essentials of her change agenda, the self-distancing work when she put up the first tableau with herself in it, and the role reversal with her arch opponents had led to more humility and benevolence. She had become capable of reappraisal, greater emotional complexity and more able to regulate her emotions when opposed.

Gale was even ready to canvass the organisation using 'snowball sampling' and find out who the hidden influencers were. She made appointments with these people and listened to them and talked with them. Some she won over, some she lost, but with all she gained a vastly wider appreciation of what made employees at Claxton's tick.

> She found that she could keep her basic positions about the changes that Claxton's needed, while appreciating others' standpoints. She also made getting the right people for the project team her number one priority. These people were not only natural allies (Gale's old way of working), but were likely to be attracted to new ideas about the business. In the longer term, she stopped demonising the opposition, and they stopped demonising her. She even came to acknowledge that her ideas might gain from compromise, and that the process of getting people on board would take time and perseverance. She would have to stick patiently to the reform agenda and weather the conflict – but not escalate it. She would stand side-by-side in the storm with her project team.
>
> Eventually, after three years, and with the progressive assent of senior management, she and her team reinvented Claxton's as a vastly different operator in the sector, highly responsive to the market, and zealots for service. They addressed and simplified the way Claxton's interacted with their customers, and reduced the costs of doing business. After three years it was clear that Claxton's had changed so much that there was no going back.

Tuning – the interface of the personal and political

We are each 'tuned' in a different way – things that disturb our neighbour, friend or partner do not disturb us, and vice versa. We can't stand noise, they don't mind it. We like lamplight, they find it gloomy – 'Let's call the whole thing off' as the song goes. Each of us resonates to our environment like a violin string to a bow. Some things clash, and some sound like a sweet song. That's where we naturally go – towards the sweet song, or at least, the song that sounds sweet to us.

It is a good feeling to resonate, to be in sync and share passion and goals with like-minded people. But who, if your client is a manager, will look after the other persons, parts or projects that are neglected? Considered this way, tuning presents a rich seam of inquiry for clients: towards whom or what does the client resonate, and what happens to the non-resonated-to? Tuning matters at work: it determines where clients place discretionary effort, and where they have little interest and as far as possible avoid.

What is the field of play? When consultants inquire about a client's 'tuning', they are looking for events and patterns that trigger a disproportionate response, such as unmet personal needs, over-responsibility, hyper enthusiasm for someone, excessive desire to please, greed for praise, tolerance for chaos, or disturbing over-comfort with conflict. Personal tuning is only one star in a complex galaxy of interactions at work in an organisation, but it does play a part in what is going on, and amply repays examination. Clients often express embarrassment tinged with relief when their personal tuning, hitherto unnoticed by themselves, is revealed. When it is out in the open it can be corrected, modified, or allowed for.

The coaching potential of tuning discoveries is extended when the notion of tuning is applied beyond the personal. Clients can also be tuned to events, programs or goals. HR leaders can be uninterested in HR, and put all their attention to their passion – OD. Or the COO is a not-so-closet visionary leader, and favours dramatic high profile interventions over the daily grind. Both of them can resonate with one project and not others, or one part of the organisation and not the rest, or one way of organisational intervention without even considering other strategies and methods. This is not to squash the life out of any enthusiasm in the company – one must be allowed one's passions – they may well translate to greatness in the organisation. Leaders aware of this imbalance can make up for their lack of tuning by delegating that section or those roles to another. Leaders unaware of their tuning can be a danger to the organisation as resources to that unfavoured side of the organisation unaccountably dry up.

When attending to client tuning on the Balcony, the Consultant listens carefully

Where do they constantly focus?
Who interests or draws them?
What do they think is 'beneath' them?
When have they been here before?
Of what are they uncertain?
Where are they bored?
From whom or what do they shrink or neglect?

Such questions help the client to connect to their own material so that they can read it for themselves. From their elevated platform they can take stock of the organisational system and their part in it. A simple way to work with this is to have the client lay out the organisation with magnets, and the magnets representing the highly tuned to can be separated out, and moved to, say, the left hand side of the board, and worked through one by one. The

Figure 7.5 Magnets on left and right side of the board

untouchables or less touchables can go on the right side. The Consultant asks the client what he or she has done/is going to do about each magnet on the right hand side – that part of the organisation that is not quite their cup of tea.

What a relief for one's dark side to be acknowledged in the safety of the Balcony! For a while, the client gets a rest from the dance floor. The height and distance of the Balcony lifts them out of the hurly burly and into a place of thoughtfulness and reflection.

Marina's New Job

Where specific persons are involved in the issue (rather than for, against and neutral to a change as in Gale's earlier case), using magnetic human-recognisable figures is extremely helpful. This will become clearer in the case of 'Marina's New Job', where Marina's tuning to particular people was central to the issue. There are some new techniques to be demonstrated, and you're likely to find some overlaps with Gale in the case above. As with Gale, the self-distancing process of the client placing herself on the map with the other people in the problem was one of the keys to the solution.

> Marina's original firm commercialised 'pure science' discoveries in the medical field. Marina had a call from Head Office. The CEO told her that the company was experiencing hard times and that she no longer

had a job. Marina, a senior microbiologist turned professional science manager, had been director of one of the company's largest labs. The CEO offered a redundancy. Marina took it, and spent the next six months looking for work. She was not successful.

As she saw it, she now had no job, no family, no partner, no hobbies and no children. Her job had been 'everything'. Taking it away was devastating, leading her to serious questions about herself. It was not just the tasks and responsibilities that had been displaced; it was also social networks.

Leaving a job, even when by voluntary redundancy, can light bonfires of emotions – dread, loss, grief, hurt, betrayal, anger, anxiety, envy and fear.

So it was with Marina. She was accustomed to managing bright people with big egos, to working with clinicians, entrepreneurs and post-docs, and to solving problems in the frenetic world of research translation. She was used to organising things. She was used to all-expenses overseas conference travel. She would do practically anything to replace her old self.

That is why, when she was offered the position of Faculty General Manager in the Health Faculty at a prestigious university, she accepted immediately. After all, she had a PhD and deep experience in research management, knew the health field, was no stranger to the vagaries of a university environment, and was a hard worker. All seemed well.

But after a couple of months, it was clear that all was not well, and she asked Corrine for help. She told Corinne about a number of factors that were limiting her ability to manage the faculty. These factors included a person in her team who was disappointed not to have been given her job; her well-liked predecessor; a respected team member who had suicided, and so on. Corinne's head was spinning with all this information and these personalities, and it seemed as if Marina was also going in circles.

To assist her to understand Marina's story, Corinne asked her to represent the players she had spoken about, choosing from a mixed set of magnets, which ranged from the coloured buttons we saw Gale use, to evocative figurines. Marina had not used magnets before, and seemed wary of being asked to do something too off-the-wall. So Corinne started her off by asking her to select several magnets to represent herself and her faculty team – the direct-report group with which she was immediately at odds. Marina did so, placing plain yellow magnetic shapes in a horseshoe configuration, but with one exception – a larger magnet of a yellow face (see Figure 7.6).

Immediately, both Corinne and Marina had relaxed. Some of the system, at least, was 'out there' and had become visible and real. Strangely,

Figure 7.6 'Nobody' and the yellows

just by being depicted, it seemed more manageable and – bonus! – it did not have to be remembered.

Marina quickly eased into using the magnets, so much so that, spying the more evocative figures on an adjacent board, she snatched up a bland stick figure magnet, and placed it in the centre of the gap in the horseshoe. Corinne then asked her to add any other figures that were relevant. She was silent for a few moments so that Marina could complete her work.

The Consultant's silence at this stage is to allow the client to start the process in 'right brain' – the non-language side that some scholars say makes sense of things through form. Form brings to notice nearness/farness, position, size, colour, similarity and so on. Asking clients to explain what they are doing while setting up is to force them into 'left brain' – the language side. But talk – language – has not thus far solved the issues, and Corinne is hoping that working in form rather than talk will bring new perspectives.

Corinne had been seeing Marina on a one-to-one basis about team issues, but please note that the protocol of silence at set-up applies also when any sort of audience – colleagues, fellow trainees – is present. Make the protagonist's work easier by enjoining the colleagues not to talk to the protagonist while she is setting up. They may talk to each other during this time, however, and that actually helps the protagonist because she does not feel in the spotlight, or that she is 'keeping people waiting'.

When Marina had chosen the figures and placed them on the board, it looked as shown in Figure 7.7.

Figure 7.7 'Nobody' and Over

Now is the time to ask the client to indicate who each figure represents. Marina says that the yellow buttons and triangles are the team, and that she is in the centre as Nobody – the stick figure. Yellow Face, her nemesis, is the unsuccessful applicant for Marina's job. He has a grotesque smile on his face. The rat is her former job. Above her is 'Dancer', the Dean of Health, and above the Dancer is Hat Man, her predecessor, the successful faculty manager who went on to a higher job at another university, and was flourishing. Everyone, except for 'Over', flourishes but her!

It was hard for Corinne to shake the feeling that there were a lot of people looking over Marina's shoulder, and indeed Marina says something to this effect when she steps back from the board and takes in what she has created.

Avoid naming the figures yourself. The images evoke different recognitions in different people, and the consultant does not have naming rights. Even if something seems entirely obvious, such as a figure of what seems to you Mickey Mouse, might be named by the client as 'Mischief' – the mouse part is entirely irrelevant. In the present instance, Corinne had been tempted to name the clown-like figure as 'Sad Clown', but Marina said that this figure was called 'Over'. It was later revealed that this figure represented the team member who had suicided the previous year, before Marina became manager. The effects of the suicide were still being felt in the team.

Another caution: not only should the Consultant avoid naming the evocative magnets – even when one of them is 'clearly' Mini Mouse or Donald Duck, or other recognisable figures, but should also steer clear of interpreting the figures once they are on the board. Interpretation is the client's job. In selecting and placing these figures on the board, the client is in a most vulnerable space, and it does not help if the Consultant or well-meaning Freuds and Jungs from the group offer their analysis of the figures' symbolism and archetypal value. When they do this, clients often feel 'violated', as one put it. This is an intensely personal space to be working in, and the visual representation makes it quite different, and more delicate, from simply talking about such matters. This more personal form of working with evocative images strips away a host of concealments, opening up drawers and prying off lids. It is not the Consultant who opens the drawers or prises off the lids – it is the client. They become extremely intent, lost in the world of images and their meanings. Their hands hover over the board like a chess player's, before they move a figure a centimetre or so. In this very quiet process, these small movements of the figures seem to speak volumes. The Consultant is quiet, the group, if a group is present, is quiet. But no one is bored.

A map of the personal tunings in an organisational issue is not only about the client's own personality, make-up, history and life experiences; it also includes the psychological and organisational forces at work on them. The coolness and self-distancing of Balcony work helps the client understand some of these forces. They more easily recognise the resources of their leadership and restraints acting on it (their 'Bandwidth', as Heifetz usefully calls it). The tableau, and the ease of changing it with the magnets, shows complex causes, effects and circular factors that are almost impossible to describe or retain in memory.

Magnetic figurines encourage the client to see things in interactional terms – 'the patterns that connect' persons, actions, feelings, events, beliefs, pressures and loyalties. Since relationships between parts of any system are reciprocal, complex and confusing, any process that can stabilise and show their two-way influence is helpful. Clients can experiment with these influences, moving the figurines to and fro, seeing the effects of nearness and distance.

> When the tableau is established, Corinne can follow with 'Tuning' questions. She asks Marina to what particular figures she is drawn or is most sensitive.
>
> Marina says that she is most attuned to Yellow Face, who is furious with her for getting the job. She says that she is also drawn to the figure of Hat Man, the person she had replaced, who had been so well-liked and competent. She felt 'utterly' grateful to Dancer for having given her the job when she was so desperate. She was hyper sensitive to Dancer's

reactions, and this anxiety fuelled her attempts to build the team and deal with Yellow Face's churlishness.

Bandwidth

Corinne and Marina now have all the important elements on the board – the rat (trauma from loss of former job) being linked with Yellow Face (her envious rival), Hat Man, (her successful predecessor greatly idealised), Dancer (to whom she owes 'everything'), and 'Over', the team member who suicided. They worked on hierarchies, ordering these figures from most upsetting to least upsetting. They ordered them again into hardest to fix to easier to fix. Marian moved the magnets around and restored them to their original place. They looked at complex and reciprocal influences, and the possible consequences or snowballs of any moves. They thrashed out these issues at length until Marina was tired of it all. The sting had been taken out by representation and repetition, so that Marina was no longer very interested in Yellow Face and his shenanigans, and no longer so excessively grateful to the Dancer, or so envious of Hat Man.

Corinne is now ready to ask Marina about her repertoire of skills and emotional competencies ('Bandwidth', as Heifetz 2009 calls it) to deal with the issues she has raised. The potency of the factors that were bedevilling her had gone, and she could draw up plans for dealing with what could be dealt with, and accepting other things over which she had little influence. Marina had been in business a long time and was a competent manager; she soon re-established her equilibrium.

Converging evidence (e.g. Kross et al. 2014) suggests that visual and verbal self-distance enhances adaptive self-reflection, especially following stressful situations. Using the scenarios made by magnets, clients can connect their thinking self with formerly dismissed or overwhelming emotion. People actually in a confusing system rarely can see all of the system – they do not see themselves as part of a system in which a mess exists, and so either blame the rest of the system, or blame themselves, as if there were an on-off switch. If inability to see the whole system is where they get stuck, a more encompassing view at the visual level is most helpful.

After three coaching sessions with Corinne, Marina was already involved in projects and actions that would help her and her team. She wasn't at all happy with her self-title of 'Nobody'. She had kicked the rat out of the house.

Bandwidth includes the techniques and personal gifts the client has for leading change. Less comfortably, it also includes the self-imposed limitations clients place on their range of responses by staying where they feel safe. So when the loyalties and tuning have been laid out, as we saw in a few cases above, what are the chances of the client being able to act differently? Can they mute their tuning to an over-tuned person (Yellow Face and Dancer in Marina's example), and can they genuinely seek to understand the conflicted loyalties of those they are trying to engage, as in Gale's case?

The Bandwidth focus gives the consultant many opportunities for coaching. Start with a series of gently paced questions like these:

I imagine you have developed quite a few strategies and skills over the years in dealing with difficult people like the ones on the board there? Can you tell me some of them?

Have you ever had to deal with a tricky character like (Yellow Face?) before? What was the outcome? Can you remember what helped and what didn't help?

Are you willing to learn of new or unvisited techniques? How might you do that? Learning something new, or practising in a way you haven't practised before can present difficulties, not only at the skill level. Before we start, can we spend a few minutes talking about what might come up for you personally if you embark on changing your responses to another way of dealing with obstacles and frustrations?

Visual depictions of the system do not only enlighten the consultant – strangely they enlighten the client too, even though it is the client who has created the picture in the first place. They have not been able to put it all together, and instead the distressing thoughts, in Marina's case, become much more than a business problem to be solved. Self-transcendence, achieved here by depicting oneself in a system instead of the system as some kind of mechanism quite separate from oneself, can be one of the steps in the getting of wisdom.

Using a simple three-part focus – Loyalties, Tuning, Bandwidth – nuances of feeling that have been previously sensed but not trusted can be expressed in the safety of the Balcony. There is time to take things slowly, to see systems, and to verbalise felt meanings. By looking at personal change and self-adopted limitations in Bandwidth, a more sophisticated and relevant approach to the client is possible. The change starts with leaders in a most personal fashion, and represents more than skill acquisition. Expanding one's bandwidth is not easy – it requires a move out of one's comfort zone to where one's incompetence may show, and one's inadequacies felt. But given the lack of progress made when remaining in one's comfort zone, it can become a preferred option, no matter how frightening.

References

Duan, L., Sheeren, E. and Weiss, L. (2014). *Tapping the power of hidden influencers.* McKinsey Quarterly, March.

Grossmann, I. and Kross, E. (2014). Exploring 'Solomon's paradox': Self-distancing eliminates the self-other asymmetry in wise reasoning about close relations in younger and older adults. *Psychological Science*, 25, 1571–1580.

Heifetz, R., Grashow, A. and Linsky, M. (2009). *The practice of adaptive leadership: Tools and tactics for changing your organisation and the world.* Boston, MA: Harvard Business School.

Heifetz, R. and Linsky, M. (2002). *Leadership on the line.* Boston, MA: Harvard Business School Press.

Kahneman, D. (2011). *Thinking fast and slow.* New York: Farrar, Straus and Giroux.

Kross, E., Bruehlman-Senecal, E., Moser, J. and Ozlem, A. (2014). Self-talk as a regulatory mechanism: How you do it matters. *Journal of Personality and Social Psychology*, 106, 304–324.

Chapter 8

The Living Room
Understand

A living room is a place to meet with others, a low-key domain to air issues or just talk, or read, or watch TV. In this porous space, quiet talk and musing can help people find new understandings and settling points. Here, the Consultant sets an atmosphere where people are willing to be inquirers, to acknowledge their uncertainty in the face of issues for which there seems to be no precedent or solution. Use this Room when you judge clients need time and space to think, and the right people to think with. Here, their public mask of certainty can be laid aside, and clarity and doubt can live together for a while.

In this chapter we will be raiding the action methods toolkit of stage, place, encounter, lines, objects, image and movement to select for special attention image, place and objects.

Peer consultation using graphic depiction

For several years now, the form of work described next has been the most satisfying of all that I do. Here's how it goes: a small group (four to ten) of senior people meet to discuss difficult issues they face. Normally these issues are not management problems for which there are already known solutions. Rather, they might be tricky personnel matters, ethical issues, competing values, sudden underperformance of a section, new and aggressive competitors, changing attitudes, and the like. Any of these conditions can set up organisational confusion with which the members of the peer consultation group have to deal. The expression 'leading in uncertainty' applies to most modern leadership situations, and it comes up in this Room quite regularly.

I will outline some ways in which the Consultant might work with such a group, in the first place using the magnetic figures that we saw in the Balcony, and then with using physical objects, such as chairs or people to represent various structures or strategies. Whereas in the Balcony the focus was on an individual leader, here in the Living Room, the focus is on engaging peers as co-consultants. Members of the consulting group can come from the same organisation, or from different organisations.

Whether the people are from the same or different organisations, take care at the start of the series of meetings to establish confidentiality for this highly sensitive work. To my relief, in many years of using these processes across many professional fields, I have never heard of it being breached.

The proposed method of graphic depiction enables each member, 'presenter' or not, to learn from each other. As does the single client on the Balcony, each participant gains knowledge of the system for which they are responsible, and their own part in that system. Collectively, they make progress on diagnosing what happens in their organisations. Together, they use this diagnosis to find ways to resolve the dilemmas and engage their people in facing what must be faced. The non-presenting colleagues greatly benefit from seeing a system other than their own, or their own system through the eyes of another. It is also common for strong bonds to develop, though this is not the primary purpose of meeting.

These groups can be run on a spontaneous 'what's come up since we last met?' basis, or on a book-a-case system for the next meeting, or both. Reserve two to three hours for the whole session. Meet regularly.

For the pre-booked turn-taking process, encourage participants to consider a situation that is troubling them, and for which they would value consultation. This situation can be an organisation-wide one faced by the whole group, or by one member when the issue is peculiar to his or her division/

team. In their preparation, presenters find out as much as possible about their complex situation, deciding what information their peers will need to be able usefully to respond. This means they have to know what is essential about their issue (easier) and how to ask for help (sometimes harder). Needless to say, asking for help is not part of the myth of heroic leadership. Doing so, and responding to peer consultation, is a new and wonderful experience for many.

The other members who are not presenting have their task, too. That task is to consult to the presenter so that he or she can see new options for action. For colleagues to be useful to the presenter, they need good listening skills, a sense of timing on when to intervene, and how to throttle back their own ambition to 'solve' the case. Cases that are presented visually lead to very strong warm-ups for the audience, who need to contain their unrequested advice and insights. This is no MBA-like case study about people one has never met – the presenter is a peer in the room, laying their professional competence on the line, their blind spots, mistakes and failings for all to see. Delicacy is as valuable as clarity here.

We make sense of the world through visual representation. Churchill in his famous Map Room used colour-coded pieces of string to understand what was happening. He realised that visualisations are efficient – even if they are only humble colour-coded pieces of string. He and his staff could quickly comprehend vast quantities of information that were otherwise too interlocked to understand. Subtleties and complexities could be depicted by proximity, colour, shape and so on, even with something as crude as bits of string.

This efficiency, speed and comprehension of complexity is also a property of using magnets on a vertical surface. Taking away the burden of memory (they look different from each other, they're coloured, they stay on the board where you put them, and do not move until they are moved) means participants have more 'brain space' to see complex relationships. They kick open insight's door, and create a shared view – everyone is looking at the same thing.

Objects on a vertical surface announce themselves as lying on a kind of 'map'. Now, a drawing or a slide does this, too. But it is quite laborious to change a drawing even when it is on a whiteboard. Here's a simple example: supposing you have drawn three circles representing three related people – Hugh, Kate and Jane – on a whiteboard. You want to show what happens when one of them – say, Kate – moves away to manage the London office. All the relationships change. To show the change, you have to rub out the first drawing and draw a second one. And what happens when Kate moves back after 18 months? Quite likely the Hugh/Jane relationship has changed, because of the move away and the return. The three circles cannot be in their original formation. You have to draw for the third time the new arrangement, having rubbed out the first two. With magnets, however, you can slide them in an eye blink, slide them again, restore them to the first place, modify that, and so on. The speed and efficiency of this process allows your clients many try-outs and options while your they search for the best solutions.

I'll now outline at length a process where 'the issue' is put at the centre of the tableau. Parkes (2005) describes a similar use by Heifetz. Please understand that this is one way to do things, but not the only way, as we shall see shortly. As you become more familiar with running a peer consulting group using magnets, the only instruction you will need is 'lay out the case using magnets'. The first time it is a little clunky, but after that group members get it pretty quickly. There are many ways to construe a problem. Please be advised: having a magnet representing 'the-issue-at-the-centre' is just one of them (but a good one).

Issue-at-the-centre method

Reader, do not worry if you do not fully get across all the complexities in the following case. It is an example only, not a set of rules that must be rigidly adhered to. Briefly, the whole set-up instruction could be summarised this way:

> *Put the issue in the centre and array magnets around it representing various forces, people and organisations with respect to the role they play in this issue. Show, sliding the magnets, how each of them reacts to or causes a reaction to others in the system. Then we will discuss all this.*

A participant, Linda, identifies a challenging work situation, and tells the group what is at stake if the challenge is not met. She places one magnet in the centre of the board to represent 'what is at stake'. The question becomes: 'How can I help the people am leading face the challenge and adapt?' This centre what-is-at-stake magnet should be prominent in colour or tone, and different from all the other magnets that will soon be on the board. It should not move during the whole process.

Conrad asks Linda what the forces at play are, coming from outside and inside the organisation that will affect the centre magnet? Such forces might

Figure 8.1 Magnet in centre

Chapter 8: The Living Room   93

be changes (and opportunities) in consumer tastes, new protocols brought about by social media, e-commerce, new arrivals in the field, changes in budgetary or tax situations, and so on. Linda depicts these too, using magnetic arrows (very handy shapes by the way – if you cannot buy them you can cut arrow shapes out of magnetic tape). Conrad asks, *'On whom do these forces land and how do they get transmitted throughout the organisation? Show these figures.'*

The simplified picture in the diagram shows only two 'forces' coming from the figure in black and one from the stick figure on the upper right. The reality is there will be more 'forces' than these operating in the organisation, but these two are new, and thus far the organisation has not found a way even to understand, far less to counteract them.

Remember, these instructions on Linda's case as outlined are not sacred text – it is simply the way one consultant worked with one client putting the issue in the centre. If you start to use this method in consulting, fields of creativity will open out before you, and the-issue-in-the-centre is but one of a hundred stems nodding in the wind for you to harvest. The magnets are not magic, and your set of them can be very basic, such as the one shown here. After all, Churchill made do with coloured string. The magnets, with their ability to stick and slide, are nothing more than a simple means for making issues and relationships clearer. They make the consulting process easier by

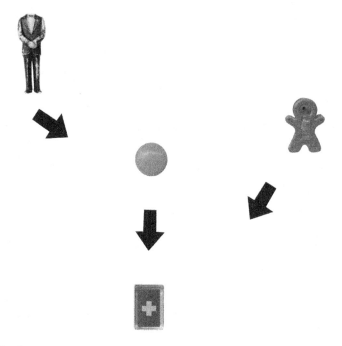

Figure 8.2   Forces at work

presenting juicy consulting points before the colleagues, a bit like a butler presenting a tray of very unusual hors d'oeuvres. There is so much to take up.

So far the matters represented have all been impersonal – 'forces' etc. Different individuals in the organisation, however, have an interest in this change, either wanting it to work, or not wanting it to work, as we saw with Gale Force. Linda arrays these individuals, a magnet each, around this centre magnet. Where possible, she is encouraged to represent them by different evocative figures. Conrad advises her to place them near or far from the centre, and near or far from each other. In this way, they form clusters that have a rationale for being put together. Don't ask the presenter about this yet.

Similarly, if different departments, groups or branches on other campuses or in other countries have an interest, display them with magnets depicting built structure, such as a castle or a house. See Figure 8.3 showing various campuses of Linda's organisation on the middle left, the lower centre and the middle right. In all likelihood, many of the individuals already portrayed are part of those branches. Moreover, there may be several factions within a department, and this also can be shown by position.

Show by proximity and/or colours any other alliances and coalitions, partnerships, and relevant interactions. It is tempting to draw on the board for this, but preferable not to. The point of the magnets is that they can slide, and the consulting colleagues may want them to move over all of the board as they try out different solutions. Having writing on the board inhibits this process.

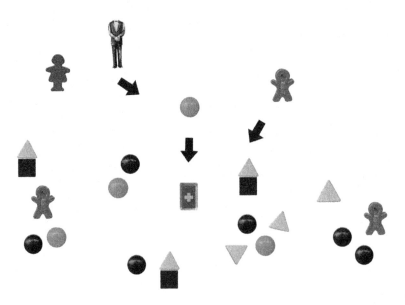

Figure 8.3 People and coalitions around the forces

When all the relevant magnets are on the board, allow the conversation to start on what to do. The real names of the various players are not needed, as participants can refer to 'Red Circle', 'Yellow Triangle', 'Black Suit', and so on. The sociometric map containing the whole field of action – which is everything in the entire whiteboard – is held and distilled, ready for analysis and action. This action may best be expressed physically – moving some of the magnets and experimenting with new relationships, bringing in counter-forces (if any) and so on.

Laying out the system, including the 'forces', does not of itself produce solutions. It almost always brings solutions closer, however, and provides scope for experimentation. There is little risk in this – the magnets forgive error, and can be moved in an eyeblink back to their original position, or to a new one as participants employ their best strategic thinking.

From the above work with Linda, and from the descriptions of individual work on the Balcony, you are by now familiar with laying out a system using magnets, whether simple counters, or evocative images. It's time to diversify and apply your knowledge. Here are some examples of what you might do.

Questions that matter

Even though the tone is gentle, and the pace easy, Living Room questions are still personally confronting. In this example, all members of the group are from the same section of the same organisation.

To start this process at the simplest level, have the presenter depict the organisation as four levels, including that of the consulting group itself, using magnets. They can be simple counters if you like.

Suitable questions might be:

- *What, personally, do you want from your Division/Team? Show this, using a magnet.*
- *What do they want from you? Depict this with a magnet. If there is more than one 'want' from the team, use several and place them next to each figure on the board, as applicable.*
- *Can you give them what they want?*

Part 1 of the question is perhaps familiar; Parts 2 and 3 not so much. Break the group into pairs to warm up to this question. This enables members to dig deep with each other and shake off some of their nervousness. Allow 15 minutes. The pairs return to the whole group. Ask a participant to go to the board and indicate his or her group. They slide the magnets representing themselves and their group, and, still standing, start with the first part of the question, touching a magnet when they are talking about an individual. When they have finished to their satisfaction, they move to Part 2 *'What do they want from you?'* and Part 3 *'Can you give them what they want?'* These are searching questions, as you can see. Attempting to answer them is greatly rewarding personally for the presenter, and there is significant collateral value in terms of the group's understanding of organisational life and its demands.

Here is another sort of question that is effective in setting participants thinking. Get agreement on a particular set of difficulties facing the organisation. Choose a magnet to represent one of those difficulties, and set out the organisation with as much detail as required, around that magnet.

> *'How have each of us been involved in creating or sustaining this difficulty now facing the organisation?'*
> *'What part have I played, if only by neglect or collusion, in this?'*

Each person comes out and in turn shows how he or she has contributed to the difficulty.

A further question, not so personal, for the consulting group could be:

> *'How do our current norms thwart or aid achieving our purpose?'*

Ask members to list the norms in their organisation. Get agreement if possible. Depict each norm with a magnet. The board can be divided into two sides: 'thwart' on the left, and 'aid' on the right. Members slide the magnets as they see fit, explaining their reasons. Sometimes it may not be possible to have a raw left and right, and a continuum might be required.

Addressing such questions highlights the complexity and paradoxical nature of leadership and change, inviting an inquiring stance as well as a problem-solving one. In this Room, complexity does not need to be hammered into simplicity. Here, people can teach each other about unseen aspects of a problem, and discover constructive ways through it.

Visual depiction

More neurons are involved in vision than in all other sensory modalities combined. The visual cortex is the most massive system in the human brain, powerful and complex, and overshadowing other large functions, including language.

So, it seems strange that visual modes aren't more common in consulting. Illuminating research from Harvard and MIT (reported by Perry 2013) suggests that faces and human-centric scenes are typically easier to remember than just about anything else. The research group collected more than 5000 charts and graphics from scientific papers, design blogs, newspapers etc., and manually categorised them according to a wide range of attributes. Serving them up in brief glimpses, the researchers tested the influence of features like colour, density, and content on users' ability to recognise which ones they had seen before.

They found that a visualisation would be 'instantly and overwhelmingly more memorable' if it incorporates an image of a 'human-recognizable' object – photographs, people, cartoons, trees, dogs, aeroplanes – any component that's not simply an abstract data visualisation such as a bar chart. A graphic (even a bar chart, apparently) with *even one* of these components has a far better chance of being remembered than one without any.

Alas, for most PowerPoint presentations: bar charts, pie charts, scatter plots and so on were *least* memorable. These forms of visual representation seldom make an appearance in memory. They often don't last – not even to the next slide. This is why there is always plenty to see in Our House, whether it is gritty 'foundations' drawn on a wall in the Basement, or a waste bin next to a chair to simulate a toilet, or laundry baskets helping a team sort its washing in the Laundry.

Why magnets?

A strong reason for using magnets is that they foster experimentalism. You can play with all sorts of scenarios and solutions without the tedium and slowness involved with depicting a constellation using drawings or graphs, and then wiping them out when the smallest change occurs. You do all that, of course, with the magnets, but it is much less onerous and much quicker. You can slide a piece if you want to, and it will stay exactly where you put it for as long as you want. You can create scenes in a trice, and delete them just as quickly.

There is no mystique to using magnetised counters or human-recognisable figures to create a shared view of complex factors. Sporting coaches now regularly employ a magnetic board at half time to depict tactics and moves, and no one thinks it odd. You, as a consultant trying these processes, need not think it odd either. In fact, if your clients are a little nervous, tell them about the reassuringly normal activity of coaches. Those men and women, in a pressure situation at half time, know that magnets stick to a vertical surface, that they take the effort out of memory, and that they allow a group of people to look at the same complex and interconnected thing (a team of 13, say, and another team of 13 opposing it) at the same time.

Using magnets to depict systems is economical: 'A picture is worth 10,000 words', as the saying goes. Sets of images cut to the chase, slicing through systemic opacities. They can show complex systems that are too large and too involved to be comprehended except visually. In assisting clients to understand complex patterns, the objects have the advantage of staying put until moved. This frees up memory while the client works on the next set of relationships. Unlike words that scoot away and disappear without trace, they are 'parked' as it were, until driven somewhere else. They snare in memory shifts of relationships at which words falter and are lost. We grasp these relationships almost instantaneously, though, when they are depicted visually.

Figure 8.4 A teacup drawn in canonical perspective

Objects on a vertical surface approximate to the 'canonical perspective' (Palmer et al. 1981). The canonical perspective is the most common one we use when we are drawing something or taking a photograph – side-on, and very slightly above. Draw a tea cup, if you want to try it – odds on it will be from the side, but showing a little bit of the inside of the bowl.

We prefer this perspective because it has maximum stability, familiarity and functionality. It contains the most salient characteristics for recognising that particular object – its 3D structure is more clearly perceived.

By contrast, the same objects placed on a low table are harder to see because of crowding around the table. You're also most conscious of the person right next to you, and that can take focus away from the scenario being depicted. Going further, placing small objects on a floor gives an almost completely bird's-eye view. Working on a floor with very small figures (as distinct from working on the floor using chairs or stools) also can have a regressive effect on the group, akin to kindergarten. Few managers will be willing to squat on the floor for any length of time – it feels too regressed, and, in any case, is physically taxing to aging joints.

Collecting a range of human-recognisable objects

It is desirable to have a range of objects – 10 to 25, perhaps – human, animal and inanimate. Some should depict the monstrous or despicable (a rat, perhaps, a cockroach, an evil-looking man or woman or two), some ambiguous or mythical figures (an egg, Barbie, the Virgin Mary, Superman, Wonder Woman, Batman, Catwoman and so on). Also useful are sublime or mystic figures, a couple of animals, a little car, a train engine, and some different-sized house-like representations (chiefly for depicting different campuses, such as head office and satellites). You'll need a few ordinary-looking men and women, drab or smart, and some cartoonish characters – Mickey and Minnie Mouse, Goofy, Bart Simpson and the like. Disney figures are not popular for nothing – they have an extraordinary hold on the 'unconscious'; they are highly evocative and often chosen. 'Mickey!' people exclaim, snatching one of them. The author has many such, but is unable to show them in this book due to copyright restrictions. This list may sound daunting, but once you get started, it's fairly easy to find objects to your taste. Shops at art museums often have superb magnetised figures.

Many of the magnetised toys found in supermarkets are not suitable, as they are highly oriented to violent characters, military folk brandishing guns, or gross-muscled figures with swords. Just one of those menacing figures in your collection should be plenty.

Though some characters, especially the superheros, come with magnet already attached, you will find that many of the best figures come simply as toys, and you will need to glue a magnet to their backs to make them stay on the board. Generally, this is not hard to do.

Physically representing ideas and systems – working in the round

Organisational language has a way of getting nods, as if the speaker and the audience know exactly what is being said. Yet, if tested, this is often not so. Physical representation, on the other hand, puts a blow-dryer into the fog, and outlines emerge into the clear. Objects – even a set of empty chairs – representing something else, allow kinaesthetic and visual modes of processing information. People representing something else add auditory modes to the kinaesthetic and visual set to which an object, even the most wonderful of magnets, cannot lay claim. When you yourself are in the tableau, the experience of being somewhere – here rather than there – comes first. Thoughts and rationalisations follow, as you attempt to make sense your position.

Malcolm's Seven Deliverables

Malcolm, a lean and ambitious Assistant Secretary of a large government department, had come to launch a two-day residential for the managers of one of his portfolios. He and his fellow executives had workshopped some new ideas for the Department, which they boiled down to 'Seven Deliverables'. It was clear that Malcolm liked these 'Deliverables' very much; he sounded stern and managerial as he read them out to the group. However, neither the managers present, nor Casey the consultant could make head or tail of what they meant, and what Malcolm's managers were actually supposed to 'deliver'.

We have seen several ways of 'making things visible', and bringing Clarity, Vitality and Alignment to teams and groups. We have explored Post-it notes, magnets, standing on a line, forced-choice performance reviews and so on. But we have not yet addressed one of the most searching ways to bring clarity to a set of organisational matters, and that is to 'concretise' them by substituting a person for an abstract idea. The advantage of persons, in this context, is that they can speak.

Casey asked Malcolm if he would be prepared to investigate a new way of representing the Deliverables. Malcolm agreed that he would try his best.

She then asked him to choose a person from the group to be each Deliverable. Malcolm selected his seven, and Casey got them to stand. Initially puzzled, but then getting the hang of it quickly, Malcolm allocated from his list a Deliverable to each of his chosen seven. When he had done this, Casey asked him to move them physically, standing them in relation to each other, and in relation to their main (internal) client – represented by the chair (you will see parallels already with the 'issue-in-the-centre' process, outlined earlier this chapter). Which one was near to which, and which were further away? Malcolm enacted this, pointing to various positions in the room, and still referring to his list.

Now Casey asked Malcolm to role reverse as each one, standing in their position, and to give an account of himself there as if he were actually a Deliverable. The first staff member, who had been Deliverable

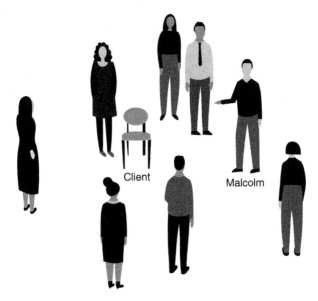

Figure 8.5 People standing in different positions around the client

#1 goes to the centre chair (the principal customer's place), and Malcolm stands in Deliverable 1's position. The staff member then interviews Malcolm as Deliverable #1. He starts by asking him who he is. Malcolm-as-Deliverable #1 struggles and looks at his notes. He reads from them; they are entirely in management-speak. The interviewer says that he does not understand. Could Deliverable #1 explain? Malcolm tries. The interviewer-as-client asks questions such as 'What are you doing that's different from the ways things are?' And so on. After some of this, the interviewer-client asks how Deliverable #1 is going to help him in his work for the Department. Malcolm struggles, but puts something together. The Consultant then asks Malcolm to become Deliverable #2, and the process is repeated.

Deliverable #3 was called 'driving excellence'. Casey asks if the 'driving' is like driving a herd of cattle, where the cattle (excellence) are in front of the team, or is it like 'driving Miss Daisy', where the team members are chauffeurs and the person or thing ('excellence') being driven is behind them, sitting in the back seat, as it were. Malcolm is nonplussed, and at last says it is like the cattle – the team is behind. 'Where are they driving excellence to?' asks Casey. Other questions followed. Casey role reverses Malcolm into being a steer and interviews him – does he know where he is being driven to? Malcolm-as-a-steer doesn't. He says, 'All of us are being driven from behind and we are just meant to go faster. Doesn't matter where.'

This, of course, is funny. But being funny is not the purpose. After some discussion, Malcolm and the team are able to unpick the intent behind these management clichés, and sort out more grounded ideas of 'excellence' and what is excellence's destination. They reflected on whether 'being driven' was the same as going faster. The details are not of our concern here, but suffice it to say that taking up the simile of 'driving' was most clarifying, and the team was able to align itself with the intention behind the high-sounding words.

When the interviews with the seven are complete, the Consultant asks them all to tell each other how they relate not just to the chair in the centre (spoke to hub), but to each other (spoke to spoke). Malcolm reverses roles into some of these positions around the rim, and Casey helps him out so that he will not lose face. The process becomes very intense.

The shift from one's own role to that of the other creates a dialectic within which insight lurks. Malcolm's move to a Deliverable had involved a temporary consent to relinquish his own self. To speak in role as something or someone else requires empathic identification with the other – after all, you are standing in their shoes.

As a Deliverable, Malcolm had found it challenging to give an account of himself in plain language. It was impossible to use corporate language now that he was out there when speaking as 'Deliverable #4' or whichever. Despite his embarrassment, he got credit from the group, who could see his struggles and who appreciated his courage. In the process, Malcolm found that he had a great deal of work to do if he was sincere in his need for the Seven Deliverables to be run throughout the Department.

> To the enduring respect of his managers, Malcolm did that work, simplified the seven to five, simplified the language of those five, and was able to say what the relationships between them were, and their hierarchical relationships with the principal internal client. He applied his new visual chart to other portfolios, and spoke plainly about interactions and paradoxes between priorities. His people were satisfied and felt more confidence in themselves and in Malcolm. As one of them remarked, 'We would never have delivered on those rubbish Deliverables, but would have stuck something in a report about them which no one, not even Malcolm, would have read, and which in any case we would have fudged. We would have just re-labelled what we ordinarily do, and not actually changed anything. This way, we've got real targets and everyone knows what they are – even Malcolm. We'll go hard at them too, because we believe they're in the long term helpful to the client.'

Physical methods in a standard consulting process (SWOT)

A company to which Corinne was consulting was at a stage that indicated a SWOT analysis might be useful. As this is a well-known business technique, I will only describe the basics here. An action methods SWOT process differs from a conventional one in that the grid is drawn on the floor, rather than on paper or a whiteboard, and participants are asked physically to occupy the various squares and take up a role. That is, every participant in the Opportunities quadrant becomes an Opportunity, just as everyone in the Threats square becomes a Threat. Corinne addresses the Opportunity group collectively as as 'Opportunity', beginning with an ultra brief warm-up: something like *'Hello, you're an opportunity are you?'*, and then proceeding to question what type of 'opportunity' the person is. Likewise, in the Strengths square, the interviewees *are* strengths.

Though similar in structure to a paper-based SWOT, the 'feel' in the action methods version is more powerful. The stakes are raised, and speakers from within a square do so with unusual passion. They also seem to come up with new material that they may not have accessed if the exercise were a whiteboard one. I have found that participants particularly relish being in the 'Threats' quadrant, as there they can let loose their inner villain with *'I'm coming to getcha'* speeches. A little of this is very lively and engaging,

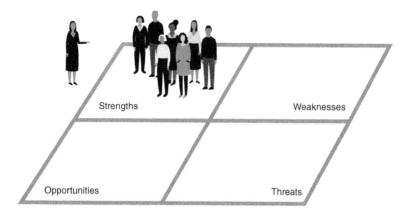

Figure 8.6 The Living Room – SWOT analysis

but it must never become farcical or your clients will suddenly stop laughing and start looking puzzled. The business purposes of clarity, vitality and alignment are fully present and must be seen to be so.

Using chairs to understand complex organisational responsibilities

In just about every consulting context you are in, there is a source of great help and it is right to hand. I am referring to chairs or stools. Sometimes, you can be lucky and there are chairs *and* stools. (Stools are valuable because they are omni-directional, whereas a chair faces one way.)

You can work with chairs that are vacant, that is, you can have one person, usually the manager, set out a particular organisational structure with chairs, and the team or group stands around the outside. Alternatively, team members can jointly set out their understanding of the structure and manipulate the chairs until they are satisfied. After the order has been set up to people's satisfaction, any time a team member has a comment to make, you can direct them to make it from a particular chair – that is, to go to that chair, sit on it, and speak.

Our next example shows one (unusual) method of populating all the chairs once the structure has been laid out.

Untangled

> Marit was Regional Director in charge of six regions in the Department of Social and Emergency Services. The Department had just undergone another reshuffle, and Marit had spent nights at the whiteboard in her office trying to determine how it would work across the large geographical regions her part of the Department had to cover – something like a

third of the size of Great Britain. The Department had demanded that Marit's focus shift to end users of the services. The portfolio across each region included Welfare, Health, Regional Employment, Ambulance and Emergency Services. Marit produced complicated charts and maps, the result of her late nights' work. No one could understand them, and Marit, an experienced bureaucrat, herself stumbled at the first questions that her staff put to her. Under pressure, she didn't understand how to bring the functional/regional mix together at ground level. 'Do you have any ideas?' she asked Celia, 'You've been consulting to government for long enough now'.

Celia did not have any ideas, and did not understand Marit's charts. She did, however, have some ways of working that had been helpful in the past. She also had an organisational 'shape' in mind that seemed more usable than any other shape she had seen.

First of all, she asked Marit what the best shape to have when a client was involved. Marit was somewhat taken aback with this question, but after a little explaining from Celia about organisational depictions and 'shapes', she said that staff standing in a circle surrounding the client might be best. Celia asked Marit to choose someone from the group to be 'The Typical Client', 'Elaine'. She stood Elaine in the centre of the room, and asked participants to form a circle, shoulder to shoulder, around her. When they had done this, Celia asked each one of them how they felt being in that position. Very few liked it, and most made comments such as 'pointless', 'suffocating', 'blind' and so on. In Celia's experience, a circle is nearly always chosen as the ideal organisational shape around a customer or client. When tested, however, people nearly always reported feelings of suffocation, aimlessness, etc. as Marit's team had done. In effect, Celia wanted participants to get the idea of a circle being the perfect organisational shape out of their minds.

'Let's try something else', said Marit. She left Elaine where she had been, and got the six regional heads into a V, three on each side, with Marit at the pointy end of the V, and Elaine at the open end. At this stage, the participants are standing. She asked each of them how they felt. Most said they felt fine, some said they were OK or would like to be nearer or further from Marit, or next to someone in particular, or on a different side of the V. Celia obliged with these swaps, until all were happy. She asked them to get a chair each, and put it where they had been standing. They did this.

Celia asked Marit what she could see. Marit said that she could see her managers and the client at the same time. Celia went to one of the managers and asked him what he could see. He said that he could see his

Chapter 8: The Living Room   105

Figure 8.7   The client-facing V

boss, his colleagues and the client all in the one glance. She tried another regional manager, who said more or less the same.

The next move was to ask the portfolio heads and deputy heads and staff in each region to stand behind their regional head. This is shown in Figure 8.8, with only one of the regions' portfolios elaborated for the sake of simplicity in the diagram.

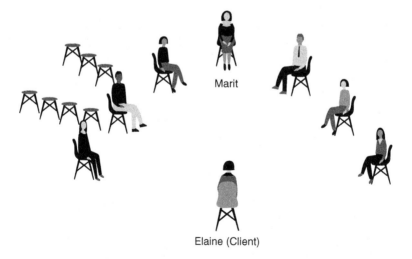

Figure 8.8   V shape showing one region's direct reports

Now Celia asked the six regional heads to get a chair from another part of the room, and his or her portfolio managers to take a stool each and find a quiet space. They would then replicate the original V within their own region and with their own clients. Naturally, there would be different clients in each of the portfolios – a welfare client, and employment client, an ambulance client and so on. The constellation of the V would change somewhat according to whose portfolio the client fitted. But no one could leave the V, because what held them together was the fact that the client was a client of the region, and therefore a collective responsibility as well as a specific portfolio responsibility.

When they have got this formation right, they can ask questions such as:

To whom do I report (i.e. is the regional head my boss or is the portfolio head my boss)?
Who sorts my workload?
Who else in this area do I need to combine with? How often?
Who in neighbouring areas do I have to co-ordinate with?
Who in other functions do I have to co-ordinate with?
Do I have two reporting lines, one for this part of my work, and one for that? – and similar questions of vital concern to those present.

In many cases, neither the regional Head nor the functional Head could answer these questions, and nor could Marit. They start to disentangle the various reporting lines: 'It's just like a fishing line that has got into a right mess!' one said. Members start to envisage how to work in new ways in their own region, and then in their own function and how, in all this, to keep a constant focus on Elaine, or her 'end user' counterpart in other portfolios.

People gather into small groups that continually shift as members finalise an answer, or have to consult another small group that might contain people that they were now to work with. Their chairs and stools stay where they were originally put, and people reference them constantly.

Celia does practically nothing. These people know their business, and the questions they need to find answers for, far better than she.

Participants got it sorted in two hard hours. Every member felt they understood how they were to work inside and, to a degree, outside their own function or region. Everyone remembered that day, a year later. Marit was very relieved.

Tip: When you have a problem of messy structure and complex reporting or 'direct line of sight to the customer' problems, think chairs. You, the consultant, do not have to know the business better than your clients – but you are expected to help them find ways to think about their business (clarity), and to be enthusiastically (vitality) on the same page (alignment). Chairs are solid – they stay put if you want, but you can move them. You can sit on them or stand beside or behind them. They're great place markers. Best of all, their ordinariness makes them acceptable to the most psychology-shy client.

Place and 'placeness'

Our sense of place and ability to navigate are some of our most fundamental brain functions. While we make meaning through all our senses, it is primitively made in the body: space interacts with us at a precognitive, physical, visceral level, so deep that it can make us shudder. Proximity and position matter to us – we feel comfortable here, and not there, OK next to this person and not to that, just right at this point on a line, and not at any other.

A sense of place (knowing where you are and how you got there) is one of the first faculties to fade in Alzheimer's. Neuroscientists have long searched for an underlying cause for this saddening disease. One of the clues was their identification of what they called 'place cells' (Niediek & Bain 2014): whenever a rat was in a certain part of a maze, a particular neuron fired. It seemed that each place in the maze had its own neuron in the rat – its very own 'place cell'. Furthermore, the cell would fire even though conditions had changed or were disguised when the rat was nearby – different colours, higher walls and so on.

In addition to our having single cells responding to particular places, we apparently have specialist grids in our brain reserved for getting around these places (Moser et al. 2015). The three key scientists involved with the discovery of place cells and grid cells are worth listening to: they became winners of the Nobel Prize in the Physiology of Medicine in 2014. They note that these getting-around grids are unique to each place. Grid cells organise the relationships of distance and direction between place cells. They also play key roles in our *experiences* of place – not just the 'where' and 'what happened', but also 'what was it like? In other words, place holds memory, and can be emotional.

When in one of the Rooms in Our House you stand in a place that represents your opinion on something, by definition that spot is different from all the other places you might take. A little neuron lights up just for that one spot, is encoded and is stored in your brain, possibly forever – 'I'm standing here, and the others are standing there'. That place on the floor becomes sloshed with memory and meaning. The opinion becomes drenched in identity – undeniably yours.

Place is a fundamental aspect of everyday life and connection between the person and the world. Sense of place is a faculty that grasps the distinctive subtleties of different bits of the world and helps us find our way around it. Our sense of place shifts across enormous scales – from my breakfast position at the kitchen bench, to the back garden of my boyhood, to the valley where our farm was. We marvel at migratory birds yet again finding their right nesting place after flights of thousands of miles. We know that marine animals, too, such as whales, travel extraordinary distances to calve. They seem to be following some 'map' obscure to us, familiar to them. I am at the limit of my scientific knowledge here, but are place cells and grids acting there too?

Relph (2015) suggests the word 'placeness' for the quality of being in a place. Placeness is a felt living ecological relationship between a person and particular place, a 'somewhere'. Place and placeness – feelings of oneself or an object being 'just right' – or horribly wrong – in terms of 'where' is remarkably subtle and complex. The more you practise action methods, whether using magnets, lines, chairs or persons, the more chance you have of seeing how utterly inbuilt this behaviour seems. You watch a client's hand hover over the position of a magnet – near, far, up down, left right, as if the world depended on it. Why are they taking so long? You see team members apparently fussing over a hidden pattern to get their exact place in it. You watch a group member frowning over the placement of a chair as they set up a scenario or an ideal leadership constellation. Like maze puzzled rats or migrating birds or pregnant whales, we know our spot, our billions of spots, and they light up when we are near.

References

Moser, M., Rowland, D. and Moser, E. (2015). Place cells, grid cells, and memory. *Cold Springs Harbor Perspectives in Medicine*, 5, 1–15.

Niediek, J. and Bain, J. (2014). Human single-unit recordings reveal a link between place-cells and episodic memory. *Frontiers in Systems Neuroscience*, 8, 158.

Palmer, S., Rosch, E. and Chase, P. (1981). Canonical perspective and the perception of objects. In *Attention and performance,* Long, J. and Baddeley, A. Eds. Hillsdale, NJ: Lawrence Erlbaum, pp. 135–151.

Parkes, S. (2005). *Leadership can be taught.* Boston, MA: Harvard Business School Press.

Perry, C. (2013). What makes a data visualization memorable? *Harvard School of Engineering and Applied Science Newsletter*. October.

Relph, E. (2015). www.placeness.com

Chapter 9

The Study
Clarify

Advantages of a team constructing and interpreting its own data

One of the Holy Grails of consulting is to help organisations gather their own data about their 'system' (their series of interacting relationships) and to make meaning of those data. *'What's there? How is it affecting you?'*

With Clarity, Vitality and Alignment as the goal, the action methods consultant devises ways to engage people in making the system more fully known to its members. The Living Report Card, described in this chapter, is one of those ways. It works with the unique perspectives, stories and concerns of the client group. Rather than a consultant collecting all the data, then interpreting their meanings and finally packaging them and feeding back those meanings to the client, the members themselves construct and interpret the data. During the process, matters facing the team should become much clearer (Clarity), and members should be highly engaged and alert (Vitality). Alignment comes in the second part of the process with the consultant assisting the manager and the team to process the material.

Of our consulting tools of stage, place, encounter, lines, objects, image and movement, we will use stage, place, encounter and lines the most in this chapter.

The Living Report Card provides a frame in which discovery occurs – where people uncover collective intentions, matched or mismatched stories about events and their significance, and shared or disputed perspectives. In the working through of all this comes Alignment. The participants provide the data that they interpret for themselves personally and then for the whole group. Their 'system', if you like, becomes open to them, and they can connect the dots: what do the patterns they have created mean, and what might be the possibilities of doing things differently?

When you are considering using the Living Report Card as an intervention, it helps to bring along a prepared list of components of effective teams, such as those from Huszczo (1996, 2004), and show these to the manager. The 'team' could be the executive group of the organisation, and therefore the 'manager' would be the CEO. Again, the team could comprise an entire small organisation – say a group of 8 to 12 people, and the team leader, therefore, is the 'boss' or even the owner. Finally, it could be a middle-ranking team entrusted with a special mission in the organisation. Max was the manager of this last kind of group.

The Living Report Card procedure: Max's morass

Max leads a Health Information and Policy (HIP) team in a large government department. He is a genial figure whose calm under pressure and political savvy was valued in the cutthroat world of public policy. All members – five women and four men – are highly qualified, most with PhDs. They have all, save one, been with HIP for a long time. Their accommodation is considered luxurious by public service standards and a tribute to Max's powers of influence. He is admired for holding on to a large space through lean times and charmingly repelling the endeavours of various razor gangs to slash bits off it. He is well-connected politically, and always seems on close terms with the Secretary of the Department, no matter who is the latest to go through that revolving door.

When Max first came to see me, he was his usual circumspect self. He wanted 'a bit of training to help people with various work-styles'. From long experience I took this as code that there was trouble in his group. He said that there were 'difficulties' possibly owing to some 'personalities' or clashes of working style in the team. This, as I later found, was true enough, but the reality was more severe.

It is often helpful when given a team-improvement job to conduct a confidential interview with each team member. Max agreed to this, and said that he would respect the confidentiality of his team members, and did not want any sort of 'report' except of the highest and most airbrushed kind. To his credit, Max always honoured this confidentiality protocol.

In these interviews I found the team to be a leaking misery of organisational life, full of real or imagined insults and offence-taking with each other. The team culture was like the slow-burning rage of peat when it catches on fire. Nearly all this peaty rage was directed at the impeccable Max.

His subordinates said that he used bullying tactics, that he undermined and blocked at every turn, refusing to impart knowledge, had no succession plan, truly believed that he was irreplaceable, played favourites, was mean spirited with feedback, micro-managed, squashed innovation, avoided key areas of the strategic plan, used a team member as an 'attack dog' who did all the dirty work, and kept people in line. They complained that he shut down any proposals that were outside his comfort zone, that he had no stretch targets, and took all the exciting and high profile work for himself. To everyone's relief, regular meetings had lapsed under this sour weight of ill will.

What was I to do with all this? How was I to bring out even some of the material, given that people were so hostile and afraid?

The Consultant's Friend – The Living Report Card – was what I hit on to help. That was how I could get every team member, including Max, to contribute publicly to a systems analysis. The Report Card is a great instrument for upward and lateral communication.

Outline

The Living Report Card takes time and thought to set up, but is then easy to run on the day. Basically, it comprises a number (from 5 to 7) of relevant components upon which members might rate their team. Participants can only award one 1, one 2, one 3 etc. up to 7. They rank the items and transfer these rankings by Post-it notes to lines on the floor. When called upon, they stand on their Post-it and defend their ranking to another person on that line who has given a different ranking. When all the lines are exhausted, much of the data have been brought out and at least some of the system (it does not usually encompass outside forces and other political and economic events), is displayed in the patterns of stickies. The data yield is very great at an individual and system level.

Sample

I used seven components with Max's group. In other sources about teams (e.g. Lencioni 2001, 2005; Huszczo 1996), you will find a smorgasbord of further components that may be useful. Don't select more than seven, though. Seven already contains a massive amount of data to be processed. Here they are:

a. Clear sense of direction
b. Efficient operating procedures
c. Constructive interpersonal relationships
d. Role clarity
e. Right mix of skills and abilities
f. Flexibility
g. Constructive external relationships

These components are transformed into a process that seems always to bring people alive and invites deep engagement. I had worked with Max on getting the right components from a list that I have compiled over the years. Part of the work is gaining agreement with the sponsor on what he or she wants to test the team. The consultant needs to have real input into this process, or the sponsor, less experienced in consulting and facilitation, may select items that do not get to the heart of the matter, or that repeat themselves, e.g. practically every item concerns interpersonal relations, or 'communication' or 'budget'. But there is more that goes on in teams than interpersonal relations, communication or budget as we saw in the Laundry. Here is a further list that might help you vary the components.

Further examples of 'report card' items to build your repertoire

Sometimes, managers are meticulous in designing items, asking for completely new items, for example 'We meet budget targets' or adjusting off-the-shelf ones to their purposes, for example 'Trouble – we handle hassles, hard times and conflict without having to look to authority'. Here are some gems from the field:

Budget – We meet budget targets.
Quality – We comply with the Quality Management System.
Clarity – Each member is clear on the part they have to play to reach these goals.
Contracts – We employ first-rate contract management practices.
Links – Finance makes strong links across the Department.

Environment – This is a good place to work.
Supply chain – I receive quality work from others.
Fit – We are comfortable working with the ambiguities of this workplace.
Accountability – Project leaders are appointed with clear end-to-end responsibility for a given piece of work.
Learning – Learning and development within the unit mostly come from being responsible as leads for projects that stretch us, and/or from gaining new skills outside our most common designation.
Trouble – We handle hassles, hard times and conflict without having to look to authority to sort things out when there is trouble between us.

Let us suppose that Max is happy with the original seven components just as you see them above, and has signed off on them as likely to yield relevant data for improving team behaviour. Label them A to G (never 1–7, as this will confuse your clients who are ranking the items on a 1–7 basis – then you would have two 1–7s – very messy!). Print them off on a single page, and have enough copies ready for everyone.

First, on the workshop day, mark seven parallel lines on the floor with masking tape. Make them 4–5 metres long if you can, and separated by a shoulder width or so. Head each line with a marker on the tape 'A' to 'G'. Mark the top of each tape with a '1' and the bottom as '7' as shown in the diagram.

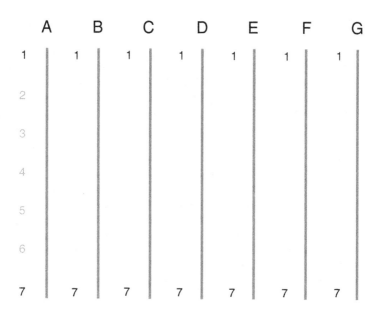

Figure 9.1 Living Report Card

Second, hand out your instructions, as below, geared to the seven items that Max chose.

Sample page of instructions to a team

Please rank each of the following items (A to G) on a 1 to 7 scale where 1 is 'high' and 7 is 'low'. Please rank every item, giving a number only once (i.e. only one 1, one 2, one 3 etc.). That is, you must use all your rankings, even if you think the team is great on everything or poor on everything. Allocate a score from 1–7. Please avoid dead heats. Write your ranking in the margin beside the item.

a. **Clear sense of direction**
   There is a shared purpose in this group; its goals and values are understood and perceived as appropriate
b. **Efficient operating procedures**
   We are efficient at planning, identifying and solving problems, making decisions, evaluating progress, and performing tasks
c. **Constructive interpersonal relationships**
   The team is good at handling conflict and, when things go wrong, sorting out matters for ourselves
d. **Role clarity**
   The expectations of leadership are well established; we understand our roles and how they fit in our organisations game-plan
e. **Right mix of skills and abilities**
   Our group has the full complement of relevant knowledge and skills to do what we should be doing.
f. **Flexibility**
   We're accustomed to leaving our usual roles and tasks and flexing into someone else's area when deadlines or Unit priorities require
g. **Constructive external relationships**
   We operate well in the wider organisational contexts, and have good relations with other groups inside and outside the organisation

Stress once more that 1 is a 'high' ranking and 7 is a 'low' ranking. If you think it helps, move to the lines, actually stand on a 1, and say 'One is up here', and move to the other end of the line and say '7 is down here'.

Third, when participants have finished their ranking on their master sheets, hand out seven Post-its, or other similar product to each participant. Prepare ahead by marking A, B, C, D, E, F, and G on each of their little pads of seven pages. Get participants to write their initial on each Post-it note. When they have done this, ask them to write their ranking on each. For example, Mitzi might give a '2' for Item A – 'Clear sense of direction', a '1' for Item C – 'Constructive interpersonal relationship', a '5' for item B 'Efficient operating procedures', and so on. She marks her seven Post-its

Chapter 9: The Study   115

(A – 2, C – 1 etc.), and initials each one. The other group members do the same, according to how they see their team working.

Fourth, have participants place their initialled Post-its on the grid lines in the slots of 1 to 7 provided. Don't be surprised that, no matter how apparently clear your instructions, people get the order of things mixed up, e.g. 7 is 'good' and 1 is 'bad'. Because the process is fairly fluid, these things can be sorted, and pretty soon everyone gets it right. When members have placed their Post-its, they sit down again.

Fifth, go to the first line (Line A: Clear sense of direction) and pick up a Post-it from nearest the top (the 1). Ask to whom the initials belong. Have that person (let us say it is Mitzi, who has given it a 2, and no one has given it a 1) to stand on the line in that spot. Walk to another place on that line – perhaps a 7 if there is one, pick up a Post-it and ask whose initials they are. Have that person (let us say it is Ravin) stand on that part of the line.

Sixth, initiate an ultra brief interview with Mitzi, asking her why she is standing where she is standing – having given her second highest score for Line A – 'Clear sense of direction'. When Mitzi is warmed up by your interviewing questions, suggest that she direct her remarks to Ravin standing at 7. Walk down to Ravin at 7, warm him up if need be, and then get him to tell Mitzi at 2 why he is standing at 7 – that is, why he has given 'Clear sense of direction' the lowest score possible. Then encourage the two parties to talk to each other (and not to you), standing on their position on the line about the reasons for their choices.

Seventh, still on Line A, sit Mitzi and Ravin down and pick up another two Post-its, ask to whom they belong, get those persons to stand on the line

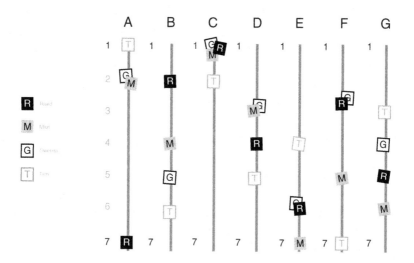

Figure 9.2 Lines with Post-its

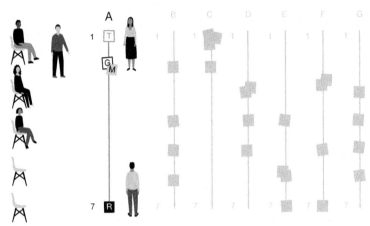

Figure 9.3 Line A populated by two participants

in their particular place on their Post-its, interview them briefly, and have each of them say to their counterpart why they are standing where they are standing. You can repeat this process as often as you like, but don't let it go on too long – it's early days and there is a lot of territory to cover. Finish the process on Line A now and park discussion for after completion of the whole seven lines.

Eighth, repeat this process with line B and beyond. It is at your discretion and the demands of time how many persons you bring out for each line – but it should never be fewer than two. It is somewhat helpful to choose the extremes (i.e. 1's and 7's rankings) for the interviews, but that can become impossible if the whole group is clustered in a 3–5 ranking for a particular item. You also need to make sure that everyone has been interviewed and has spoken at least once, and that no one – unless the group is very small indeed – has been asked to speak on the lines more than, say, four times.

Please note that when you have finished two to four formal interviews on any one line, you might choose to address the whole team and invite anyone else who wants to have a say on this item – 'Clear sense of direction' – and ask them to take their position on the line. Don't allow speeches from their comfortable seats in the audience. Actually standing for a position is important. You need to watch the clock, though, as you have a lot to get through.

After you have worked on all the lines, and sufficient data are gathered, leave the Post-its stuck on the floor where they are, and give the group a short break. When the members come back, the visual data are still there to refer to. Participants now sit in a circle around the lines. The Consultant asks the Manager with which line he or she would like to start the 'what-do-we-do-now?' discussion, for this is the stage of planning some changes in the light of the data vividly before them. Imagine the Manager selects the 'Clear sense of direction' line – line A. The fact that it has scored fairly poorly, and that the reasons for and against this low score have been canvassed in the earlier session by at least two people explaining their views, provides a platform for the whole group to request the Manager for more clarity, and for the Manager to explain why he or she cannot be clearer - structural reasons, perhaps, or because her immediate bosses are still working things out.

The large data yield provides opportunities for a great deal of work for the consultant and the team leader and team. All the lines, not just the ones on which the team has given itself a low score, are open for reflection and reform.

Why go to all this trouble?

The data mining phase as already described assists two modes of perception: the visual perception of pattern – the constellations of Post-its on the floor in the Review, and the 'what do we do now?' session. Everyone can easily see, for example, if a particular line is loaded at the high or the low end, or in the middle. This perception is stronger than if one had put the pooled results in a table, or even a graph. The resting places of the little Post-its representing people's opinion about an item make 'Truth' a set of relationships rather than something absolute. Participants are highly engaged in this process of discovery – they have played an active part in it themselves, and now have leisure to see the visual patterns that their collective decisions form. The 'what do we do now' question is alive and in the room, and the participants are lit up inside by discovery – 'this is what I make of things in this group, and that is what everyone else makes of things'.

Even richer data, however, have come from being in action, slight though that action is: the participants stand at various positions on the line and speak their piece. For a few moments they are on some kind of stage, in a business-oriented sociodrama, if you like. As well as seeing their position on a given item, they feel it physically. Their colleagues and boss learn not only their position, but why they have taken it up. No one is silent.

At the same time, the process is collaborative. Members of the group, two at a time, publicly discuss why they have given a certain rank to an item. The individual speaks within a community of peers, supporting or arguing with others. Apart from the questions that deal with leadership (e.g. 'clear sense of direction'), many items on which they comment concern how they themselves as a group operate. In other words, they are 'marking' themselves. Later, in the 'what do we do now?' phase, they may go into how they can collectively 'fix' certain items that they have deemed important.

Last, the process promotes high levels of autonomy. The daunting experience of standing on a line representing the rank one gives to an item can nevertheless be exhilarating. One literally 'takes a stand'. That stand may or may not be shared by others – there could be several Post-its next to one's own, or none. Even if one does have a kind of virtual 'support' in that most of the group has chosen a similar rank on this item, the process of standing alone and having one's say to a person who has chosen a different ranking is bracing, and produces new modes of communication within the team.

Advantages of physical methods of data elicitation

CLARITY: A forced choice, rather than, say, marking a 1 to 7 point Likert scale, prevents participants from scoring every criterion in the middle – a 3, 4 or 5, yielding a mush of uninterpretable organisational soup. The point of the Living Report Card process is to get a variety of opinions by people speaking courageously, then to debrief into the 'where to now?' action phase after all the lines have been explored.

By the pattern of Post-its, the group has a strong and present read-out of where it stands on a given dimension, what it does best, and what it does not do well. The data are there on the floor before the group's eyes; they have heard others and spoken themselves about their rankings. The Consultant now has plenty to work with.

Living Report Card processes are direct, rich and vivid. That makes them memorable. Individual positions are clarified when participants stand on the line and justify their stance. One can remember exactly where in a room one stood, and who was next to them, and who opposite. The experience is gouged into memory by many pathways: physical, sensory, visual and verbal. This gives them a greater chance of longevity than if these answers were merely verbal. You've stood there. Your positions stay in muscle memory: tangible, visible, clear – and they matter.

VITALITY: Because vision and movement involve right brain as well as left-brain, they can lead to different solutions. They employ different 'grammars' and therefore propose different questions. Participants are not only surprised by what others say, but by what they themselves say. Even though they may have prepared an 'answer', this answer is likely to leave them once they are standing in a particular position in a room, and new information floods in. Enactment increases desire to self-disclose. Propositional knowing (one has already marked the card) is prior to experiential knowing: it's different when you get out there on the line – you experience at the physical level a choice you have already made at the intellectual level. Your body responds to the place you are in – a 6 on line D. Somehow, you have an almost uncontrollable desire to state your case – which in this moment seems like stating your being. You are a 6 and not a 1 or a 3.

Even the simplest dramatic act – standing on a line – produces a frisson not easily equalled by filling in a questionnaire or voicing an opinion as an 'audience member'. In standing on a line, in standing for what we mean, we subjectively and emotionally experience our histories (see A Walk down Memory Lane). Our views are right up against us as we take our stand. Even though the matter might be a minor one, we experience ourselves as choosers, with our existence somehow 'on the line'. We're 'taking a stand', as the saying goes.

The forced choice and the edgy politics create an engaged and vital group of participants. They're active, rather than passive, energetic, rather than aloof or bored. Whether you are the speaker on a line, or watching someone else who is, you're more present than if listening, or half-listening, to people sitting and talking.

ALIGNMENT: This experience of 'being on the line', of feeling one's existence, of heroic consciousness of oneself as a solitary, responsible chooser, is often a transient one. On several lines, one's identity becomes dynamic rather than fixed, and more social than personal. Closeness, position, similarities and differences, bonds and divisions are the very meat of sociometry (Moreno 1953; Treadwell et al. 1998). In giving my ranking of 6 on the line representing 'Clear sense of direction' I am like others who gave 5, 6 or 7, and unlike those who gave 1, 2 or 3. As I take up dialogue with someone standing in a different place, 'Truth' becomes relationship, and my opinion not an absolute, but part of a network of ideas and views.

The Report Card does not of itself produce alignment, but it does show it by the pattern of the Post-its. The reflect-and-repair sessions afterwards, if successful, will produce the alignment, especially around 'Clear Sense of Direction' and 'Role Clarity'. The effect of doing the exercise itself, of living through the affinities and separations and existential aloneness brought about by the process, also generates bonds that may be stronger than before.

Further uses of lines

A line is a powerful shepherd of separation and contiguity. It indicates where a person stands, and who with. You may have noticed Claude's work in the Basement where Engage's staff were adamant that they preferred to 'work together' rather than alone, and often did so. In these instances, the stress was on the length of the line, and one's position on it. In this short section, I would like to discuss the line in a different light – as a barrier or threshold. The expression 'crossing the line' is as common as 'lay it on the table', and both are ripe for consultant harvesting.

Typical 'crossing the line' instances might be organisational behaviour questions, such as bullying, office affairs, sexual harassment and the like. I had one the other day at a hospital when 'escalating up' was the issue. When could one escalate (without appearing to be alarmist, naïve, impertinent etc.), and when should one escalate (when failure to do so would constitute neglect, lack of compassion, dereliction of duty, etc.)? How to manage this as an action methods consultant?

The answer: Get physical – produce the line! This physical production of a saying or abstract concept is called 'concretisation' in psychodramatic circles. It means, 'to make real or particular, to give tangible form to'. So if someone says 'there is a wall between Marketing and Sales', a concretisation would be to construct a 'wall' out of chairs or people, and then to interview one of the participants as the wall – *'Why are you here? What job are you doing and for whom? How long have you been here?' 'Is there anyone here that could get rid of you?' What would they have to do to?'* and so on. Sounds corny? Not when you're there – it is a powerful process, capable of bringing great insight.

Simple line methods

You can draw your line on a whiteboard, but it is far better to manifest it with a two-metre piece of masking tape (always carry a roll) on the floor. The process from then on is to take 'cases' that test the line. Participants can even write the cases and place a label representing them on the floor immediately above or below, and 'way above' and 'way below' the line. Having the 'line' physically represented adds grip to the process. Participants can then debate the position of each 'case' and where it should be. They can take notes of the principles governing 'aboveness' and 'belowness' and how to manage when something is over or 'above'.

CASE 1 – PATIENT NEGLECT

The senior manager to whom a case should or should not be escalated sits to one side of the line, and the cases are on the other. They are moved, short of the line – no escalation, and over the line – should be escalated. When all have reached agreement on the cases, it means that an escalation 'policy' has been worked up through both sides, management and staff. Everyone has a good understanding and agreement about what is above and below the line, and of the grey areas. The 'policy' – really a body of understandings – won't come down as a set of rules and a pretence that there are no 'grey areas'.

CASE 2 – BULLYING

Concretising the 'line' also works well with bullying and harassment. Various 'cases' are constructed or remembered, and people test whether an interaction is to be regarded as 'bullying' or not. There is probably a larger 'grey area' here than in the hospital escalation scenarios, where a patient's physical wellbeing was at stake. In bullying scenarios, not only the actual words or actions come into play, but other factors such as tone of voice, gaze, and so on. Use live actors from the team to enact the statements. For example: *'Have you submitted that report yet?'* can be said in a polite tone, and in most workplaces would not be construed as 'over the line'. If it is said by the actor in a stronger tone, it may. If it were shouted, it has a good chance of being over the line. And if a fist is banged on the table right next to where the participant is sitting while the person is shouting, it surely is. Get from the team other cases, and test them for being *'over the line'* or not. The end result from taking four or five cases and trialling them through various contexts, gender mixes, tone of voice, duration, repetition, etc., is likely to be a more nuanced but stronger sense of what constitutes bullying in this workplace. And everyone has contributed to this understanding.

Similarly, with sexual harassment issues, tone of voice, organisational context, gender, gaze, and 'feel' make a great deal of difference to a 'compliment'. The scene: the staff cafeteria. The personae: two people, male and female standing with their trays, waiting to be served. The man looks at the woman, and remarks: *'nice top'*. This 'compliment' takes on many shades. Is every comment on appearance over the line – that is, forbidden to be spoken in any context? If not, what isn't forbidden and what is? What is the tone of voice? In what fashion and for how long does the man look at the woman – a glance? A stare? An ogle? A leer? What is the wider setting? An insurance company? An IT start-up? Does the nature of the workplace, e.g. very hierarchical bank with a large HR department vs very flat community service – make a difference? What is the organisational position – the power hierarchy – of the wearer vs the complimenter? Does that matter? Create the line on the floor, and have the two participants (to lessen discomfort in the role play, preferably two men, with one playing the man and the other the woman) say the words in various ways, and for different lengths of time, emphasising the gaze, tone of voice, physical distance, and so on. After each enactment, participant audience comment and debate, moving the role playing couple one side or other of the line, building a code suitable for their workplace. Again, this is a compelling way for a team to work out its unique protocols, especially in 'grey areas', for a desirable organisational culture in their own industry.

But please, however you do it, portray the line. It's so simple. Put the tape on the floor, and start. The very minimal dramatic or psychodramatic element of physically representing the line makes all the difference.

Live Leadership Review

Leadership reviews, such as a 360°, can play an important part in a manager's learning path. The trouble is, they are usually debriefed in great privacy with the manager's manager. The 360° review is under-used at the group level, and is almost never 'live'. Yet, with a willing senior management group, led by the CEO, an organisation can learn to be open about matters formerly considered private. Openness becomes the norm. In this process, the manager knows who has rated her on what, and has been able to ask 'Why?' On a conventional 360° this opportunity is rarely given, and a manager must simply put up with the feedback without knowing who wrote it or what they had in mind when they did write it.

You can create a Live Review on almost any criteria that are seen by the organisation as important. The example below contains five frequently cited elements of leadership adopted by one company I worked with. They called them the 'Must Do's'.

Method

Hand out a sheet of paper headed 'Five Criteria of Leadership'. Write the criteria of your choice – the ones below are an example. There is no shortage of books claiming to have found the essentials of leadership reduced to three, five or seven 'key' elements – use them if you like. Best of all, though, employ the client company's own published leadership framework if they have one.

Meet with the manager in question a week or so beforehand and tell him or her what you are proposing to do – that is, they will be publicly rated on the company's leadership criteria by their subordinates.

Note: You absolutely cannot spring this on someone: it is not nice to embarrass a person, and not even ethical to put someone unwarned on the spot as this process does. In any case, it will fail if the client is in danger of losing face. His or her subordinates will sense it and close ranks to protect him or her, question you at length, not understand the instructions, or find other ways of making the process founder and flop. Your manager has to be keen, even though nervous, to do this. You are likely to have had a strong and trusting relationship with this manager, and he or she will be accustomed to your ways as an action methods person.

That's about protecting the manager. As for protecting the group, do not do this process with a manager who is likely to pay out on his or her subordinates after the session is over. Generally speaking, a manager who welcomes this process, albeit nervously, is not likely to be one who exacts spiteful retribution afterwards.

Prepare a set of instructions along the following lines and hand them out to the group.

Five criteria of leadership

Please circle the number on the scale below that you think best fits your manager/colleague. '1' indicates that your manager is very well described by the sentence, so far as you are concerned; '5' indicates that your manager is not well described by the sentence. You may not use a number twice; that is, you may only use one 5, one 4, one 3, one 2 and one 1.

Communicates a compelling vision	1	2	3	4	5
Builds in stretch targets and goals	1	2	3	4	5
Makes people accountable	1	2	3	4	5

Provides meaningful feedback   1   2   3   4   5
Brings out the best in people   1   2   3   4   5

Place five substantial posters on the walls about head-height around the room, each one with a number on it, from 1 to 5, written in large letters. Why substantial? Why large lettering, when a small piece of paper, or even an index card, could be seen just as well?

The large signs: 1, 2, 3 etc., add to a sense of drama. The big papers on the wall contribute to making the whole space a 'stage'; participants will be standing and moving through the space. On a stage, things are a little starker, a little nearer the bone. There is theatre in rating one's boss out in the open, but none when one sitting in one's own office anonymously filling in 360°. Once again, standing in a particular place adds to the sense of making a choice, of standing for one's opinion.

When each participant has finished marking their own paper, approach a person (let's call him Joe), and ask him what he has scored his manager (let's call her Monica) on item A: 'Communicates a compelling vision'. Joe says that he has given Monica a 4. Ask Joe to stand under the poster with a '4' on it. Once the rest of the group has seen what you have done with Joe, they 'get it' more quickly. Ask all of them to stand up. Then ask them to move under the poster with the number they have awarded Monica for Item A. Typically, there will be a scattering of scores, but sometimes several will gather under the one poster, signifying a consensus on that item.

Monica is standing in the centre of the room and the group is now spread out under their chosen posters. Ask her to approach any one of them. She asks that person (let's keep using Joe as our example): 'Joe, why did you give me a 4?'

Joe and Monica then dialogue briefly, with Monica mostly listening, and only questioning to clarify something that Joe has said that she did not understand. She does not justify herself or try to argue with Joe. When she is satisfied that she has understood the reason for a 4 that Joe and his colleague

Figure 9.4   Leadership posters 1 to 5 on wall

have given, she interviews Jessica, also on a 4. Then she moves to another poster, let's say Poster 5, where there are two people standing. She interviews them, and, still on item A, she visits each of the poster sites and interviews the person or persons standing there.

This process is repeated four more times until the manager is ranked on all five items, and, if the group is small enough, has had a conversation with each person on each item.

It is most likely that when rating the manager 'low' – a 4 or a 5, the rater will say that they only did so because of the forced choice, and that of course the ratee is excellent on that dimension too: 'I only gave you a 5 because all the other numbers were taken'. The Consultant intervenes and says something like 'Nevertheless, you did give a 5 for this and not a 1. What is your reasoning? Why not a 1 instead of a 5?' Courageous managers, Monica in this case, who are the subject of the feedback might say something similar themselves, and not need the Consultant to intervene. They want the data. They understand the forced choice (which protects the rater from political payback or fallout later), but are still interested in the relativity of the scores and the reasoning behind them.

This is an exercise that not only involves the manager receiving feedback, but group members practising giving it. The Consultant ensures that this is so, by asking the member to re-phrase or to provide specific instances if he or she has not been sufficiently specific, for the feedback to be useful.

Note: it is possible to reverse this process, by the manager giving the group feedback on a set of dimensions – it could well be the same set, if the members of the group themselves had direct reports. If the group in question were a single-level team, the criteria could be the values of the team or group. It could be on components of a single dimension – let's say 'accountability'. Once again, five (or whatever number is relevant) posters are stuck high up on the walls. This time it is the manager who has scored each dimension, using the same forced ranking process. The group starts in the centre, the manager – why don't we use Monica again? – stands under a poster, let's say one with '3' on it. She asks the group to move towards her, and for them to question why she has given a 3, say, for item C: 'Makes people accountable'. As before, they may not dispute what she says, but can ask clarifying questions. When item C is done, the consultant asks Monica to move to another score, and the process is repeated until all are done.

Living Report Cards, whether they take the team form as we saw with 'Max's Morass', or the individual form, as in the Live Leadership Review, call on courage and vitality from all involved. Somehow, in all the times I have run them, there have not been 'political' ramifications after the workshop day. This is partly because everyone seems to understand the forced nature of the rankings, and that they will have to speak about things that are not going as well as they might. I have not seen anyone use the lines or posters as a place to grandstand or pay back. The Living Report Card, a little complex at set-up, seems to provide a safe container for troubled groups to express some of their concerns, and can sure help the consultant understand what is occupying the team when he or she comes to the repair phase.

References

Huszczo, G. (1996). *Tools for team excellence*. Palo Alto, CA: Davies Black.

Huszczo, G. (2004). *Tools for team leadership*. Palo Alto, CA: Davies Black.

Lencioni, P. (2001). *The five dysfunctions of a team*. San Francisco, CA: Jossey-Bass.

Lencioni, P. (2005). *Overcoming the five dysfunctions of a team*. San Francisco, CA: Jossey Bass.

Moreno, J. (1953). *Who shall survive? Foundations of sociometry, group psychotherapy and sociodrama*. New York: Beacon House.

Treadwell, T., Kumar, V., Stein, S. and Prosnick, K. (1998). Sociometry: Tools for research and practice. *International Journal of Action Methods*, 51, 23–40.

Chapter 10

The Attic

Remember

Use the Attic program when you suspect that the past is stalking the present, and needs to be outed.

What the consultant hears about the past is not true. But no one is lying. The past is a fugitive, always on the run. Don't try to understand its demonisation or idealisation too directly – stories take all before them. Awkward contradictions are shrugged off. The door is shut in your face.

The unique intervention here – Memory Lane – is a consulting process sitting on the back of a set of facilitation skills. These facilitation skills are not insignificant: they require the authority of a ringmaster, the aesthetic of a choreographer, and the hypnotic powers of an illusionist. The facilitator as

Ringmaster/Ringmistress, for example, keeps order in a process that could otherwise get messy. She marshals people to come one by one into the line, gets them to tell their story and that of the organisation, cuts them off when they have spoken too long, but does so without their losing face or their connection with the event. Don't worry if you do not think of yourself as a particularly whip-cracking sort of person: Ringmasters and Ringmistresses crack whips in many different ways, and you will soon find yours.

The Illusionist inspires a group of people to enter unfamiliar psychological territory where they subscribe to the conceit that space represents time. The Illusionist materialises departed or dead persons, suggesting they are sitting on a particular chair; he or she then helps group members to have conversations with them, even though they are not there.

The Choreographer sees to it that the line retains an aesthetic, and, through just-right shifting of emotional and spatial gears, allows the story to be told. If the Ringmaster or Choreographer are too passive, people tend to drift and wobble – bad news if you are maintaining the notion that space means time. If the Choreographer is too active, people will feel pushed around, and they will push back.

Here's what you're asking: participants have to walk down a room up to 12 abreast, pausing as each new member comes on board to hear their take on things, slotting them into their patch in time, and having them think all this is the most natural thing in the world, truly connected to their business issues.

That's the facilitation side, or some of it. Of our essential toolkit of stage, place, encounter, lines, objects, image and movement, we will be using place, lines, and movement the most. We have not mentioned role very much so far, but it will put in a big appearance here.

Memory Lane – a process and a training

This is both a training chapter and a Room to which you might take your clients for organisational memory work. You do need to practise the techniques therein so that you feel comfortable when you are managing several people at once. Start by directing a few single-person lines, then perhaps two persons together; with these smaller numbers, the Ring Master and the Choreographer do not have to do so much. Walking a group Memory Lane can produce unforgettable moments. At the 'business' level, it provides a reconnection with the group's character, energies and purpose; members gain an intimate understanding of the cycles that have transpired in the organisation, and that are affecting them still.

Memory Lane is a time-based inquiry using physical movement on a line, and a role-based interview at each stopping point. It is more complex, deeper and has more impact than a simple 'time line', which could be drawn on a whiteboard or a sheet of paper. We will go through what you need to do, building from the simplest form – working with a solo client – to what's at play with two people, and then with larger groups (up to 12).

The interviewing foundation is the same for all, but managing a dyad or a group brings complications that are not there with a lone client. That is why we start with an individual and build up. Physically walking a line or stepping on imaginary stepping stones is not such a novel process. Making it an organisational intervention with dyads or groups is possibly unique.

Don't be surprised if this work, apparently slight, dunks people deep in personal/professional places. There is plenty of talk on a Lane, but the talk is propelled by experiences beyond words. There is talk, but it is not essentially a 'verbal' process. There is movement, but this is not dance. There is a kind of stage, but this is certainly not 'drama' nor even psychodrama.

Memory Lane for a single client

The context of a Memory Lane for a single client is often decision-making. In the two cases reported below, both clients had to make a career decision. The first is an open-ended process, using as many steps as Lottie, the client, wants. The second client's – Mala's – life is 'chunked' into four parts, and she is limited to four steps. If you can master the Memory Lane process with a single client, managing a dyad on the Line is not such a big leap. And from a dyad you can go to a small group.

Not so fast. Let us first visit Lottie, and then Mala, so that the basic process is well under our belt.

> Lottie has asked Corinne to assist her to make a decision. She is a senior medical officer who has been offered a big new job involving a turn-around of a large hospital department. She has already managed a significant turn-around in a smaller unit, and has earned a name for herself as a person who can sort things out. This new job will be of a different order, involving large numbers of staff and radical cultural change.

Here are some guidelines that Corinne used to conduct the process with Lottie:

> **Location:** Clear a long path somewhere – you need at least 5 metres, but 8 to 10 metres is wonderful. A small office will not do, but a large conference room, or hallway/corridor, so long as it is private, is OK.
>
> **Consent:** Obtain the person's permission to join with you recalling significant events in their life.
>
> **Outline the process** you intend to use.
>
> **Inform** them that walking along a line representing events is different and often stronger than simply talking about memories.

Offer them the **'Pass Rule'** – that they can bail out of the entire exercise at any time. Tell them also that they can pass over a particular memory or time if it does not appear to be in their interests to recall it. This can take the form of not mentioning it in the first place, or saying something like 'Skip – don't want to go there'.

Direction: Stand with the participant in the centre of this long space and ask them to point to the end of the path which is the present: *'This line represents your professional life till now, but I don't know where is the past and where is now. Point to the end that represents us here now, and the other end will be the past.'*

(Please note that as well as open Lanes, the time-based process can be initiated with individuals or groups around particular themes. A themed Lane for an individual might be *'Educational Turning Points'*, or *'A History of your Relationship with your Industry'*. A themed Lane with a senior business group might be *'Our Strategic Blunders'*, *'The times we got out of Trouble when we were in a Jam'*, *'An Operational History, Good and Bad'*, *'Our Occupational Safety Record'* and so on. This way, the group can plot business successes or blunders over time – an invaluable exercise.)

There are two good reasons for this pointing process: first, you the Consultant probably have your own mental picture of which end of the line represents 'the past' – and may nominate it thus, while the client with his or her own spatial orientation may be thinking that the opposite end represents the past. If you offer *your* idea first, it is likely that the client will try to fall in with your idea, and then have to work against their own inner image of which end represents the 'then' and which the 'now'. This orientation clash will make the work clunkier as clients continually adjust to suit the Consultant. They are trying to get inside *your* picture, whereas you should be trying to get into *theirs*.

Second, when clients point to an end, they are already saying 'yes' to the process – that is, they agree to suspend disbelief and treat a floor as 'time'. Asking them to point on the present/past axis acts as an embedded command: 'Treat this space as time'. When clients do point, they effectively say: 'Very well, I'll buy that – that's 2010 up that end, and this end is 2030.'

Where to stand: Move with the client to the beginning of the line – in this case, a spot representing their earliest memory for the topic. Let's say for this client, Lottie, it is: *'Quitting in frustration my science degree when I am 19.'* Corinne stands beside Lottie, shoulder to shoulder about 12 inches away facing up the line – a little like they are both in the front seats of a car. Nearly all of us are highly attuned to other people's faces – we need to be for social survival. If Corinne were to stand in front of Lottie, her own face carries a great amount of social data for Lottie to read, and reading the Lottie/Corinne relationship is not the task here. Corinne would also distract Lottie if she stood directly behind her: it's too creepy. Lottie would feel vulnerable and worry about what's going on and what Corinne is making of her. Standing beside clients allows them to visualise what is in front (the future) without distraction. They don't have to think about their relationship with the consultant, but they can, if they wish, check it with peripheral vision.

Interview: Begin the Interview for a Role. This comprises questioning the participant so they warm up properly to the event. Let us suppose Corinne and Lottie are standing on Lottie's third step: her graduation from medical school when she is 24. Corinne begins by greeting Lottie as an entirely new person, even though it is already Step 3 and she has spoken to her on Steps 1, when she threw in the towel of a science degree, and 2, when under the influence of an aunt, she battled her way into medical school. Corinne will keep interviewing Lottie as a 'new person' every time she takes a step.

Corinne: Hello, it's your graduation day.
Lottie: (a bit doubtfully) Er, yes.
Corinne: How old are you?
Lottie: I'm 26!
Corinne: Oh, 26, eh? Is it morning or afternoon?
Lottie: (Pause) It's afternoon.
Corinne: And where are you?
Lottie: I'm on the steps of the Great Hall.
Corinne: What else is here?
Lottie: The place is full of people getting photographed. But down the steps, looking up at me, and crying, is my auntie.
Corinne: Why is she crying?
Lottie: For all the opportunities she never had – in her day people from poor families didn't get to university, far less med school ... and for me, I guess.
Corinne: Why for you?
Lottie: Because I pushed through and picked up after I had quit.
Corinne: What are you wearing today?
Lottie: A new dress, and my academic robe with some kind of sash thing.
Corinne: What colour are your shoes?
Lottie: (looking down, delighted) They're red!

With that last comment – 'they're red!' – and the act of looking down, Corinne can assume that the warm-up is adequate and that Lottie is sufficiently in role for her to inquire why this scene is significant. As the Lane progresses, she will not need such elaborate interviewing to establish the role; she can short cut it if she's sure that the client is in an 'as if' space of being a different person in each time period. In the example below, Corinne goes more or less straight to the assumption of a new role by a simple 'hello':

Corinne: Hello, you're about 29.
Lottie: Oh hi there – that's right.
Corinne: Who's here with you?
Lottie: My sister and my new boss – I've been accepted into rheumatology, but I've also been asked to take on a leadership role in the hospital – more of a management thing.
Corinne: What are you experiencing right now?

Moving across a floor that represents time or intensity is a strong and strange experience. It brings on an increased self-disclosure that is full of surprises – even to the discloser. Prepared speeches are abandoned. All that matters is this one moment in movement. The Consultant assists that moment to shimmer, and stops it sliding away to the dark. Participants find themselves at points in their life that they never thought they could visit again. Everything is different when you get out there on the line; experience takes over. You are rolled in memory like a fish in breadcrumbs.

The role of the interviewer

Note that Corinne always speaks in the present tense. When Lottie also speaks in the present tense, Corinne can be pretty sure that Lottie is warmed up and fully experiencing the role of herself as a 29-year-old. The best questions tend to be concrete, e.g. for an adult person being interviewed in role as a child you might ask: *'What are you wearing? Who is your favourite teacher? What time of day is this? Who is sitting next to you in school? Who is your best friend?'* These questions often produce extraordinary jolts of memory: all of a sudden they 'see' the person sitting next to them in Grade 3. They are there, in that classroom with Mrs Marini. Yet the role of the interviewer is deliberately flat, akin to that of a journalist's neutrality – jus' want the facts ma'am – the story of the person's life: *What is happening here? Who's around? What are you experiencing?*

The air of naïveté in the inquiry can sometimes be helped by the Consultant giving the impression, Colombo-like, of being a little slow of wit. If the Consultant is slow witted, he or she evidently needs help, and who but the client is able give it? If Consultants are too clever with their questions, too 'psychological', too omniscient, the reaction can be a shutdown. It's frightening to stay open. Whereas if, on account of a Consultant's dim-wittedness, they don't understand something, the client will help them understand. Strangely there is even a name for this in journalism: reporters apparently call it 'creative bumbling'.

A further word about the stance of the neutral person, or 'journalist': personal histories are themselves beautiful and satisfying, even though the life so far depicted may contain great sorrow. Clients are struck: 'Here is my life; this is what it is'. They are touched by their own history. An unadorned Lane is emotionally moving perhaps *because* it is not cloyed with sentiment or conventional sympathy. The purity and restraint shown by the consultant can lead them both to, for want of a better word, a 'holy' place, the very starkness of which seems to add rich and sacred meaning. It is like being confronted with a set of black and white photographs taken by a gifted photographer: they put the viewer straight in touch with the beauty, nobility and wretchedness of the human family.

Walking through time gives coherence to personal or organisational history – fragments of experience align into a picture, shards of memory merge into an interpretable mosaic. For the clients, the process has a trance-like quality – memory comes from nowhere, and plays a little jig. They dance. This is a seemingly innocuous method – after all, who has not heard of a timeline? But when you are actually walking it, events rear up like old dance partners, and your heart can burst with wonder.

Extending from the present to the future

A Memory Lane does not have to be limited to past and present, but can extend into the future. You can represent the alternatives by gesturing an imaginary fork in the road, or by building one with masking tape to represent it more concretely. Have the client go to alternate futures as depicted in Figure 10.1, asking them to create one future if they continued on their present course, and another if they went on a different path.

> Through walking the lane up to the present, Lottie's personal/professional history becomes more firmly anchored. The many steps she has taken build to a larger narrative, as she selects events that show her to herself what sort of person she is, what gets her going and what stops her, what she is like in adversity, and so on. She and Corinne now move to her professional future, and the two options are opened out as 'forks in the road'. She experiments in each, with Corinne impartially conducting the interview-in-role, and allowing her as many crosses to the other side as she needs. Eventually, Lottie chooses the big job. Corinne tests the decision, reversing her into each of the two positions and asking her in the one: *'Any regrets in taking up this big new role?'*, and in the other: *'Any regrets in not taking up the big new role?'* Lottie explores likely regrets in each option, but stays firm with her decision and within a month accepts her new position, and thrives.

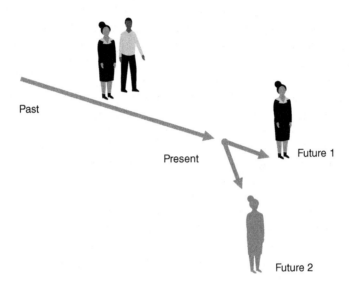

Figure 10.1 Two different futures on path

Short form with an individual – 'chunking' time

Another way of conducting Memory Lane is to determine ahead of time the intervals between each step. This can produce gripping in-your-face immediacy for clients as they select the most important events or learnings in a given period. There are also operational conveniences in the Consultant being able to stipulate the number of steps and thereby control the time that the process takes. So it was with Mala.

> Mala is in her mid-thirties, a bouncy, confident and successful financial services manager. Corinne had only two sessions with her, and was working against the clock towards the end of the second session. Because of what Mala had told Corinne about her work situation (she was unhappy at work, and was considering leaving) in the first part of this last session, Corinne needed to 'tie up' Mala's history so that it, and the choices she was about to make, made sense to her. The time pressure meant that Corinne was not able to allocate the unlimited step process that we saw with Lottie. She decided to 'chunk' Mala's past and present life into four periods of a decade each: 1–10, 11–20, 21–30, 31–40, and to add a fifth 'chunk' 41–50, a decade that had not even begun for Mala. The second part of this rapid process of grouping by decade (it took about 15 minutes) is outlined below when Mala has just come into her thirties. It is therefore Step 3.

Corinne: Take another big step (She does). This is your thirties, the decade you're in now. What's driving you?

Mala: I get married when I'm 30, I had a job with GrowCon for three years, kind of fixed that up a bit, and now for the last two years I'm here.

Corinne: What's happened to sport and dance and running and gym?

Mala: All gone except gym. I'm going three times a week.

Corinne: Will you be here (at this company) when you are 40?

Mala: (Hesitates) I think so – depends a bit on other things. Like, well, just a few things. I'm not totally happy here, and my boss is chaotic – she's driving me crazy.

Corinne: (Sensing that the years 33–40 are important ones for 'other things', doesn't press.) Now take another step for your decade between 40 and 50 (she does). What's happening?

Mala: (Looks amazed.) I'm running my own business. It's a business about business – consulting to small businesses about process, management, budget – that sort of thing (she continues with a rich description, speaking in the present tense, of what she is doing in her yet-to-come 40s).

A year later Mala described that brief session as the reason that she had stayed with the organisation. Five years later, she is still there, and happy with her *work and even her boss. The 'other things', alas, have not eventuated.*

Taking a step produces a frisson not easily equalled by filling in a questionnaire or voicing an opinion in a focus group. In standing on a line, we stand for what happened, and emotionally experience our histories. We experience ourselves as choice-makers, as owning our histories, as 'being on the line', of feeling our existence.

The experience is memorable, almost tattooed on the mind. If others are present on the line, you can remember exactly where in a room you stood, and who was next to you, and who opposite. Your own answers to a question, and those of others, are gouged into memory deeper and longer than if these answers were spoken or written. Enactments on lines are active, rather than passive, engaged rather than aloof, energetic, rather than sad or bored. You are totally present. You do not forget.

'Turning points' and reversing through time

Once the end of a Lane (the present) is reached, there are many options: you can just stop, sit down together and debrief. Or, if there is time, clients can slowly retrace their steps to the beginning, so that they have the experience of walking backwards through time, from the present to the past. This weird and thrilling process also applies when conducting dyadic or larger group Memory Lanes.

In a two-person Lane, the pair can turn around and walk back through time, as you saw previously with a single person – Lottie. The Consultant can ask the pair to pause and mark, let's say, three 'turning points' each on the way back. Here, the critical issue becomes the difference between event and time of one partner's turning point and the other's (they can, of course, be identical, but this is rare). For example, two partners in a law firm might have quite different catalysts for an event when they made a crucial decision about the firm (to leave it, to grow it, merge it, to subdivide it, to internationalise it, and so on). The actual difference in external events that triggered these decisions is often vital data for the other partner. The Consultant does them a good service by thorough interviews on why this event became a turning point. Such an interview raises valuable information for the listening partner on the other's thought processes, emotional state, and story about the event. The two of them are there on the line with a consultant or coach because something is going wrong with the firm and they want to fix it, or because they are planning a major move, such as a merger. Having a handle on each other's dominant narrative and trigger points can save them serious mistakes.

In an organisational Lane with up to ten people, the turning point process is similar, but a little more complex because of the numbers. Starting with the participants in the present, ask them to select the three most important turning points. They have to go into a huddle to determine and agree on what they are. They then walk to each of those. Conduct the interview at each turning point, using questions such as *'Why is this one such a life-changer in your team's history?'* or *'Standing at this point, what decision are you now making about yourself and the Division?' 'What future do you foresee as you make it?' 'What part did teamwork play, or fail to play, in this event?'* The appropriate questions are difficult to stipulate in advance, but will come to you when the parties are there. The spot itself, where they are standing, will prompt them.

An organisational variation is to take participants through the past and present day into one of two or several futures, asking them for input, and pointing out any inconsistencies with the group's history so far to where they want to go in the future. Have members stand on the various futures, so that they get a feel for them. Cross-question them vigorously.

Process for two persons

Two parties involved in a Memory Lane process can explore their relational dialectics in the context of time. The pair can be two partners in a business, two colleagues in a workplace, or two former equal colleagues one of whom is now the other's boss – in short, any pairing that might profit from an exploration of their history together. These processes can bring up feelings that have been long tucked away, like old singlets in a dresser.

The procedure for two persons is similar to that described above for an individual, with the following exceptions:

The parties need to agree with each other which end of the line represents the present and which the past.

Each party is interviewed at each step. The first step might cover where they met. The Consultant stands 'at the shoulder' of first one and then the other person being interviewed, crossing over each time. Let us say that the two of them both started as new graduates in Accounts at Acme Press, a mid-size publishing group, some 12 years previously. They have both moved through the ranks, and now Miriam is MD and Belinda is CFO. Things between them have become difficult and the tension is affecting executive meetings. After the usual caveats, pass rule etc., Chris, the interviewer, starts with them on their first day:

Chris: You're both new here, eh? What do you make of the place?
Miriam: It's a bit of a dump, but the people are bright and friendly.
Chris: (crossing over to Belinda's side) What about you, Belinda?
Belinda: Yeah, same. But it's a flat structure, so there aren't as many promotion opportunities as if it had been more like a pyramid.
Chris: What's the next step – the next significant change in your relationship?
Belinda: Miriam gets promoted to Team Leader.
Chris: (to Miriam) Is that the next step for you?
Miriam: No, before that, Belinda gets really sick, and I am worried about her.
Chris: OK, let's go back to that time, then, when Belinda is sick.

Figure 10.2 Moving from past to present

Under this rubric, a step for Miriam becomes a step for Belinda as well. They cannot move on to the 'team leader' step until Belinda's illness, and Miriam's worry about it, is explored. Indeed, the exploration of why something is 'a step' is at the heart of a dyadic time-based interview. Therefore, do not look on disagreement about whether or not an event is 'a step' as a disaster. On the contrary, such disagreements house the richest material. There will be many points on the continuum where an incident was insignificant for one, but major for the other. Exploring those points of difference in history leads to much greater understanding of why the parties are where they are in the present. Time rules a timeline; Belinda does not have to come round to the view that her illness was a significant step for herself – only the news that it was a significant step for Miriam, and why that was so.

In summary, the two-person deviations from a solo Lane are: (1) decision on direction must be joint, (2) interview in role each 'side', (3) chronology rules everything, (4) rejoice in disparity of memory or significance, (5) a step for one is a step for each, (6) if at all possible, get to the end in a single session, and (7) be a journalist with an interest in human nature.

Don't be too much of a 'do-gooder' while the parties are on the line. Their history is their history, and the best favour you can do is to help them lay it out, good times and bad, so that their lives become intelligible to them. There is great comfort in this bookending: *'We began there, and here we are now. This is us.'*

Working with small organisations or teams

Clients who want to make structural changes – such as merging – frequently experience difficulties no matter how well the changes had been planned, and how compelling the business case for it. Let's see how a merging example might be worked through.

> Miranda, a partner in a large legal firm, had made it to the top by putting in the hard yards and the long billable hours that the firm required for anyone to achieve partner status. The rigours of a combative legal system, not to mention home-grown dogfights within the firm, are normally sufficient to knock any vestiges of psychological thinking into the 'too fluffy' bin. Miranda was not in the least fluffy, but she did know a disaster when she saw one. She found the gloom and chaos of her recently merged department difficult to endure.
>
> Miranda's firm had decided to merge its Corporate section with its Taxation section. Miranda was put in charge of the operational side of the merger, and of 'making it a success'. She had indeed put the two groups together some six months previously, but no one could call the new entity 'a success'. She told Chris about the poor team dynamics between the two merged sectors – Corporate and Taxation. She described relationships between the two groups as 'disengaged at best'. With many misgivings, Chris agreed to take the brief.

Issues of culture and subculture arise strongly whenever two companies merge or one company acquires another. In merging cultures, the manager in charge of the merge may well attempt to blend the two cultures without openly accepting one of them as dominant. This well-intentioned wish seldom reflects reality. In an acquisition, it is a little clearer: the acquired culture usually becomes a subculture of the acquirer. In either case – merger or takeover – the problems of blending and assimilation are compounded by the fact that the two units do not have a shared history, and it is likely that one party will feel inferior, threatened, superior, angry, or permanently 'out of the loop'.

Chris had only one day to play with, but hoped that in that time he could make an inquiry into the philosophy and style of each part, their technological origins, their basic assumptions, their ideas about hierarchy and authority, their heroes present and departed, and their beliefs about their mission. He knew that this was ambitious.

In deciding that Memory Lane might be the appropriate intervention, Chris was faced with managing not one but two groups at the same time. Moreover, the two groups reportedly did not think well of each other, and Chris doubted whether they would have the patience to listen to each others' corporate stories very sympathetically or for very long. Their restlessness and low boredom threshold would give him a management problem if he were to engage with the whole staff. He told Miranda that initially he would only work with the Management team, thereby cutting the numbers to about eight. He said that he was prepared to partner her in later work with the staff at large.

> The Taxation people came from an Accounting/Law background. They were introverted, clever, and detailed. Their work required dogged patience, scientific rigour and hours of solo document searching. The Corporate people – the larger group – were from a Law/MBA background, and by temperament were more extroverted. Their culture and processes reflected this: high energy, pugnacity, meetings cancelled or changed at short notice, emphasis on winning clients and getting the billing out. The Tax people were error-averse, whereas the Corporate people were hot-blooded and buoyant. They regarded themselves as 'the chiropractors of big business', clicking a corporate spine here and there, and realigning the company skeleton. If their interventions failed, they would click the spine back to where it had been, and 'clip the ticket again on the way out', as one explained.

Participants in a merger often have little idea even of their own history and how it has translated into practices, orientations and customs. They have even less knowledge of the story of the other group.

Since an organisation's life history keeps unfolding in the present, drawing that history together helps members understand why things are the way they are. This in turn can provide a basis for decisions about how to be and where to go next. History's influence extends to people new to the organisation who were not present during the time of many of the events depicted, and who may know nothing of them. Nevertheless, they are recruited to certain narratives as representing the 'truth', and history becomes current culture. Unknowingly, they act it out.

> In Miranda's group, the Lanes depicting the two cultures were certainly not sentimental journeys, and it was fortunate that Chris was not expecting much in the way of emotional expression. He worked quickly, and emphasised event and fact, throwing in an occasional cultural and interpersonal question. The historical process, bare-boned though it was, did allow each group more clearly to see the difference between their own culture and history, and that of the other group.
>
> Chris started the process with the Corporate people in one corner and the Tax people in the other. Taking the longest serving member from Corporate, he asked questions about culture and practice and relevant major figures in Corporate's history. Next he took the longest serving Tax person, and ran similar questions. He then interviewed each of the others in turn, crossing from side to side after each landmark step, interviewing, and proceeding to the next step when the standing group have moved down the room. Eventually, he had the two groups on a single line in the present. (See Figure 10.3.)

Back to merging: when the two histories of the former entities are put physically together, side by side, participants often have little epiphanies. I say 'little' to avoid the impression that burning bush experiences are just at hand, and that the Consultant heroically leads the participants to hitherto

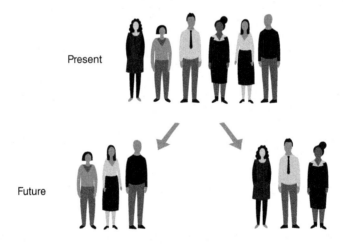

Figure 10.3 Demerging in a law firm

unexperienced areas of reflection and change. The Consultant *wants* to do this, tries to do this, and engages the techniques most likely to do this; but in tense merger situations the results are likely to be more modest. One can reasonably hope that participants on both sides achieve some sense of empathy: they see and appreciate that the merger, so uncomfortable for them and their own group, is also felt as an intrusion by the other. They may even get to the point where they realise deeply that each group has to make compromises if their workplace is to be a happy one. This is a very good point to get to indeed.

> Chris sensed it might be worth taking the merged group into the future, and this is how he did it. He asked them to form three cross-section pairs, and discuss how they saw the group developing over the next four years. After about 20 minutes he called them back and asked each group to present their predicted future. He selected a point in the room that represented a date four years from then. He asked each pair to instruct the rest of the group as to where to stand.
>
> Their projections were practically identical: the merger was so unsuccessful and the unhappiness so great that at some time in the future – in most cases about 18 months – senior management couldn't bear the reports of misery any more, and agreed on a demerger. This scenario had never been expressed before. Memory Lane had brought out the hidden fantasy: 'If we behave badly enough and seem unhappy enough, they will liberate us from each other and we can go back to being how we were.' This meant that the more disengaged the groups were, the greater the chance of 'success' in their desire to divorce. Under this rubric, attempts by Miranda to make them happier were bound to fail.
>
> Miranda's task was now most difficult. She had to convince them that no matter how unhappy they were, they would never succeed in persuading senior management that they should become two divisions again.
>
> Chris became Miranda's coach for several months on this issue, and eventually the matter settled down and the parties became more cordial. But each group never lost its prime identity, and never quite gave up hope of a demerger that would liberate them back to their former habitat.

Working with a larger group – cultural exploration

Organisationally, the past can be remembered as a single person – 'Monster' or 'Saviour'. Though they have long left the building, their lineage lingers. lying across the present. It's as if they're still here, watching, hovering, checking.

In a group Memory Lane, the basic procedures of interview-in-role, and moving step by step are similar to working with a dyad. But the increased complexity that greater numbers bring may require that some of the dyad protocols need to be set aside. For example, 'a step for one is a step for all' can apply to a very small group (say, three to four persons), but can be a burden when it is larger. There simply is not time to hear everyone's steps, and participants get physically tired standing in the one position while one or two people dominate the narrative. Management of the numbers and time becomes paramount.

Order is the main issue in working with a large group in the Memory Lane format. The basic interviewing techniques and the notion of orderly movement through time become more difficult when there are more people to cater for. Here are some ways of reducing the messiness with many people to manage.

Work beforehand with your sponsor (the person who commissioned you), finding out the sequence of current members' arrival to the team. If the sponsor does not know this sequence (they could themselves be a new-ish staff member), get participants on arrival to arrange themselves in a continuum from 'longest serving to most recent as workers here'. Place chairs along one side of the room, and get the group members to sit on these in order of their entry to the team or organisation. Place the longest-serving at the back of the room and the newest members towards the front (with higher numbers you have to give up the 'pointing the past and present').

Start with the person who has been in the team longest; that is the one sitting in the chair nearest the back wall, and interview him/her in role. Spend more time on this person and the next two or three than you will be able to with subsequent arrivals. The early interviews help the still-seated people get the idea of the timeline, and you can move much more quickly after the first few.

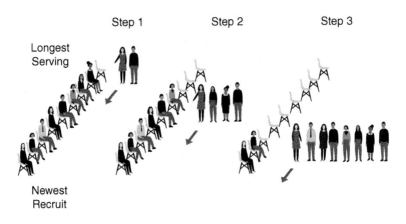

Figure 10.4 Longest serving to newest recruit

Chapter 10: The Attic   143

When members mention a significant person who has left the organisation, bring out a chair for them, and if appropriate have an empty chair dialogue (Blatner 1996; Williams 1989, 1995) between that person and the people who are still here.

Chris: (pointing to the chair) There she is. There's Beatrice. What do you want to say to her?

Jorge: You were a wonderful team leader and the place just isn't the same without you.

Chris: Tell her what was so wonderful about her.

Jorge: You just had this fantastic gift for making things work, never front on, just going round the back way, having a word with someone who was sulking that made them smile, asking about people's weekend, covering up for someone who did something hopeless . . . . Covering up for me when I was hopeless.

Chris: You owe her, eh?

Jorge: I sure do.

When the dialogue is finished, upend the chair on the floor (shocking!) and leave it there in its position (let's say the group is up to 2017 when Beatrice left). The overturned chairs on the floor help to give a dramatic time perspective. There might be one at 2012, this one at 2017, and another at 20XX. Do not produce a chair for everyone who has left the team – only for those who are significant, and who appear to play a part in the present. For example, some members may not accept their new boss, Bruce, because they are still mourning for their old boss, Beatrice. Beatrice is worth a chair.

But it is not only arrivals and departures that the Consultant is searching for. It is the lost stories, or the stories held by a few and dismissed or forgotten by others. 'Kicked out' is a good example of this.

Kicked out

Morgan is the Director of a small cardio Unit at St Jude's, the State's flagship hospital. Five years previously he had been recruited (ahead of Don, the existing Deputy Director) to take the team into the next level of advanced contemporary practice. The team is bitterly split between Morgan loyalists and Don loyalists. Fear seeps in under the door whenever they have a Unit meeting. Meetings themselves are strangled, laboured and short. Complaints about Morgan being a bully have been made to the hospital Exec. They were proven unfounded. The Unit is shunned by the cardio fraternity across the state, and colleagues say that they would not send a relative with cardio problems to St Jude's.

I was engaged to see if reconciliation were possible between the two factions. After a series of team meetings, I decided an organisational Memory Lane was indicated, though given the extremely restricted emotional climate in the team, I did not hold out high hopes for members even to participate.

They did. The walk began conventionally enough, and people obeyed the protocols of seating themselves in order of arrival at St Jude's cardio, and making comments on the culture of the Unit at the time ('Wonderful place to work, harmony, ability to exchange ideas and respectfully challenge' etc.).

When the parties came to the time of Morgan's appointment as the new director, I expected a storm. That did not happen. But two steps later when they reached a critical point (I won't go into detail here) the furies were unleashed.

Naming this incident, hitherto unnameable, was a watershed.

The group moved on down Memory Lane after this, pausing to interview new arrivals, asking them what drew them to cardio and St Jude's, differences in culture between previous workplaces and their current one, and so on.

Even though there had been only limited heart-to-heart talk between the protagonists, they had been able cautiously to smooth some of their more obvious differences.

In the unexpected and spontaneous lies what seems like the 'truth', an 'epiphany' – a sudden apprehension of the world. Elusive lines of connection, till now written in invisible ink, darken on the map we thought we had. Past actions make more sense: this is connected to that, and to that, and to that. What had seemed accidental or coincidental is now traced, placed and patterned.

The walking group moves down the room getting larger and larger until it comes to the present when there is no one left sitting. Each person that joined the line has been interviewed.

Options

When the walkers have arrived at the present, a number of options are open.

The walk can be terminated there, and people sit down and discuss what has happened and what needs to happen.

Or, you can play with elapsed time: have the members slowly (still keeping their line) move back to their original positions. Symbolically, they are moving back through time. At the start of the session, when they moved forward, they gained people from the side wall. Now they move back, shedding people as they go, pausing at the overturned chairs, which they reinstate to upright, and returning to the first point where only one person – the original member – is standing at the back wall. The remainder of the group are seated along the side wall, in order of employment, as they began half an hour previously. You can ask them to come down the room again, without interviews this time, siphoning up members from the side wall, growing until it reaches the end, and on the way once more tipping over the chairs that had been righted. In swishing back and forward through space representing time and events, the process becomes more familiar, and the past less 'hot'; it does not burn so much when one has physically travelled it two or three times. When history has lost its heat, participants are more able to think calmly about the effects of their past on their present culture.

You can play with future time based on extrapolation from what they saw worked or did not work in their history. Participants talk among themselves and commonly come up with several ideas. When it looks like there is some consensus about one of them and how long it will take to set it in place, ask the group to step forward as a body into the time they nominated (let's imagine eight months), and then recommence interviewing. Note in the example that the Consultant establishes a linguistic 'willing suspension of disbelief' by asking questions in the present and past tense, and avoiding future tense:

Claudia: (To one) Hello, it's July 20XX. I hear that you are having regular group meetings now and that it is OK to disagree with each other.
Person 1: That's right, I suppose.
Claudia: You suppose . . . what does that mean?
Person 1: Well we argue quite a bit now, and it's hard to remember what it was like before.
Claudia: (To another) Well, what is it like, actually? Was there a slow start that got stronger, or did it start with a rush?
Person 2: No, it started with a rush, but not the next meeting after that consultant woman left. (Laughter.) There was a bit of a spat one day about a particularly unimplementable suggestion, and we looked around and no one was lying dead on the floor even though we'd argued. (All laugh.) So we kind of thought that we might actually survive a bit of criticism so long as it wasn't sarcastic or coming from a nasty place – still hurts, though, if it's your own idea that's getting hammered.
Claudia: Hammered, eh? Quite a strong word.
Person 2: Well, it probably isn't quite hammered, but you still go 'ouch' when it's you. We're getting used to it, and people are pretty respectful when they make a comment disagreeing with an idea. But we do get it how dispute is actually helpful in getting good ideas to go forward, and that really rocked us, 'cos we always thought that you had to be nicey nicey and just accept everything anyone says as being incredibly brilliant and precious even when it was rubbish.

Claudia: Did you have to change any thoughts about work itself to make so much difference?

Person 3: We really had to get across the idea that our industry was a competitive one, even though we are government. Gregor (Group Director) has been saying it for ages, but we never got it. Now we're starting to look at services in other Departments that already are being put out to competitive tender, and it's making us nervous, I can tell you.

Person 4: We had to realise that we can't just take ages about a decision. When someone comes up with an idea now that might have legs, Terri (team leader) gets a small group to take it off line, thrash it out, and bring it back to the larger team when they have put it through the grinders to see how robust it was.

Claudia's questions assume that the group is actually in the future, in July of 20XX, looking back over the intervening time. She uses tense to suggest this: e.g. 'I hear that you are having regular groups meetings **now**', or '**Do** you have to change any thoughts?' She has also helped to promote this illusion of entering into the future by a physical move, that is, by getting them all to advance by at least one big step beyond the present.

When the future-time interviews are complete, Claudia could have moved the group back to the present, re-interviewed, and then to the future again, so that the new desired state is more sharply contrasted with the current state. There are many consulting options, once one has the technical process of interview-in-role under one's belt.

Consultants are not engaged to provide people with a riveting psychological experience. Claudia's facilitation means was to service an organisational end: to make use of the memories, insights and recognitions unfurled in Memory Lane as a mainsail to propel participants' productivity. That is why, while moving people around in time, her questions implanted suggestions about business in general and the team's business in particular.

Grief is not always about losing a beloved person. Grief can be triggered by losing a way of doing things, or losing an idea of what work means socially in the twenty-first century. So Claudia, speaking in the future-as-present, asked whether members had to change their thoughts about work itself (such as from a more 'wet' to a more 'dry' view), or whether brainstorming in its traditional form is helpful, or whether people can have respectful but robust relationships at work, or whether it is OK to challenge ideas, even if it hurts the proponent a little, and so on. There are many points on a Memory Lane, whether it goes into the future or not, where a consultancy intervention may be made. There are data aplenty, freely available to the Consultant and participants.

Given the ringmaster and choreographic work involved – timing, bringing people on line, keeping them level with the month and year, enticing the shy and tactfully shutting down the uncontained speakers – a group Memory Lane process is not recommended for groups of more than 12 participants. However Corinne has developed a successful way of working with large (30+) groups. As in her individual work with Mala where she preordained the number of steps and 'chunked' time, she assigns participants into 4 to 6 groups depending on date of first start in the company. The 'longest-serving' cohort meets at the back of the room, and the 'newest' at the front. Each group builds a collective story of the era when they started. Members stand in place when their time comes, and tell their story, stressing changes, achievements, obstacles etc. – in other words culture and climate. They take their seats again when they are done. Effectively, each group acts as one person telling the tale of their decade or time chunk. While not quite as powerful as the Memory Lane described above, very moving and meaningful narratives do emerge, time and order can be kept, and fatigue reduced.

Remembering is a process of evaluating and inference, rather than simple retrieval. Remembering is not a photograph. The cases reported above make it clear that no matter how neutral the consultant tries to be, the participant's 'memory' is influenced by the consultant's frame for questions, how interested the consultant is in an event, how much weight they give to it, what tone of voice is used, the consultant's gender, the group's gender mix, how the instructions are given, the process adopted, and so on. As co-creators of knowledge that is only apparently the participants' own doing, the consultants are in it up to their necks. They cannot not be. Because of this factor, participants' 'histories' are participatory realities, galaxies of subjectivity with a near infinite number of factors influencing each other.

References

Blatner, A. (1996). *Acting in: Practical applications of psychodramatic methods.* New York: Springer.

Williams, A. (1989). *The passionate technique: Strategic psychodrama with individuals, families and groups.* London: Routledge.

Williams, A. (1995). *Visual & active supervision: Roles, focus, technique.* New York: Norton.

Chapter 11

Goodbye, Keep Going

From reading this book, and perhaps from trying out its processes, you know by now that the comforting simplicity of a house conceals an elaborate set of OD interventions. The framework's apparent whimsy only intensifies clarity and the choices your clients must make. The world of work is cast in an energising, but unusual light. While the methods may appear overly playful before you start, they are not so slight once you and your clients are inside. With action methods, you are always **put through** something. Participants are not observers – they are players, making choices and standing by them.

Which brings us to risk. Action methods make us think and feel, and we do not do either of those well when we are too comfortable – or too anxious. The frisson a participant gets from, say, making a stand on a line to give an opinion, versus sitting behind a desk to do so, carries a greater sense of existence, of risk, of life. The exhilarating wave you ride can indeed be the same wave as the one that dumps you. That need not stop you from surfing; but it could stop someone in your client group. Be careful and watch your clients for distress – the apparent simplicity of standing somewhere on a line, or taking part in a role play, can be just too exposing, just too much for someone. Find a way, without their losing face, for their quick exit. Make it clear from the start that the pass rule will always apply.

As with actual physical houses, in Our House there is always the possibility of renovation or addition. That means that you could invent a brand new Room, such as a **Gymnasium,** or repurpose an existing Room, such as the **Dining Room** to meet client's needs. One consultant I know uses the whole House, all the Rooms at once, for organisations dealing with fiendish complexity and needing multiple lenses. It works! When you have a working relationship with the house in these pages, try next door, build one yourself.

The power behind Our House consulting comes from the use of simple components - stage, place, encounter, lines, role, objects, image and movement - within a specific "room". These components are the building blocks of the experience that helps business thinking. They make issues clearer, brighter and more personal; they surface solutions not previously seen. And they are there, at hand, for you to experiment with.

As you start to practice, you will appreciate more from the inside the hidden forces of the intervention you have chosen and the Room in which it is set. You'll get a feel for the basic chemistry of action methods - what interacts with what, what binds, what enriches, what soothes, and what transcends. If you work with your clients inside some of these Rooms for a while, following the set-ups as given here, you'll soon be able to improvise and adapt the work to your own style. Just as experienced chefs can make up dishes from what is at hand because they deeply understand cooking, your deep understanding of action methods, gained by practice of the recipes in this book, will allow you to adapt what is at hand, and to find 'the essential ingredient'. The more you use action methods, the more your practice will deepen and your organisational interventions will invigorate your clients – and yourself. Go well.

Index

360° reviews 121–122

action methods: adapting 149–150; chairs and stools 103–107; foundation pillars 25–26; Laundry 36–37; Lay it on the Table 53–66, 73; Memory Lane 128–147; place and 'placeness' 107–108; role reversal 77–79; and room size 54; SWOT analysis 102–103; thinking and feeling 149; as tools 4–5 *see also* continuum line activities; drama-like activities; lines; magnetic shapes; visual activities
advance preparation 44, 48, 49
Alignment 53–66, 100, 103, 109–110, 119
alliances 33, 66, 73, 74, 94
allocation of participants to Rooms 10
altruistic punishers 46–47
anonymity 11, 17, 33–34, 35
Appreciative Inquiry 22, 63
Attic 4, 127–147

Bain, J. 107
Balcony 4, 67–88
bandwidth 86–88
Basement 19–27, 73
Bedroom 15–16
Blatner, A. 143
blue sky projects 15–16
'bookends' 9, 138
boundaries: of decision-making, setting 9, 17; for sensitive material 15
brain science 8, 46, 83, 96, 107, 118
brainstorming 11, 16–17, 146
bullying and harassment cases 120–121
business model generation processes 22, 23

canonical perspective 98
chairs and stools 103–107, 143

change management 68, 87
Choreographer role 128, 146
Clarity 49, 53, 100, 103, 109–110
collective unconscious 56
common enemy effect 24, 26
concretisation 119–120
conditional co-operators 47
confidentiality 5, 90, 111
conservative tendencies 45
Consultant role 5
continuum line activities: examining the foundations 25; Laundry 35–36; versus line as barrier/threshold 119–120; Memory Lane as 142; organisational norms 94–96
corporate language 61, 99, 101, 102
cracks 23
creative bumbling 132
creativity 3, 16, 17, 149
criticism of ideas, inviting 17
'crossing the line' 119
customer service 16, 18, 66

data, teams' own 109–119
debate and dissent, encouraging 11, 17, 54–56, 61, 112, 118, 120
debriefings 63, 121, 135
Dining Room 53–66, 149
disruptive churn 8
diversity, ensuring 10
drag 40, 43, 44
drama-like activities: Balcony 73, 78–79; foundation pillars 22–23, 26; Living Report Card 114–116, 118–119, 120–121, 122–123; Memory Lane 135; in standard consulting processes 103; Toilet 40, 48 *see also* interview-in-role; stages (theatre-like)
dreaming 15–16

effective teams, components of 110
efficiency 7
elimination 31, 39–51
emotional competencies 86
empathic identification 101
empty chair dialogues 143
experiential versus propositional knowledge 118

face, saving 61, 101, 122, 128
facilitation skills: Attic 128, 146; Basement 25; Dining Room 60, 61, 64; Study 112
feedback 11, 124
floor plans 2, 9
Foundation Inspection process 22
foundations 3, 19–27
fundamentals 19–21

game theory 24
Garbage 49
Garden 14
Gintis, H. 47
grid cells 41–42, 107 *see also* matrix boxes
growth 4–18, 40
Gymnasium 149

habitual thinking patterns, disrupting 8
Heifetz, R. 68, 71, 85, 92
hidden influencers 70, 79
homework assignments 10
horseshoe-style layouts 18, 44, 58, 61
human-recognisable objects 23, 81, 96–97, 98–99
Huszczo, G. 110, 112

identity 40, 107, 141
Illusionist role 128
influencers 70, 79
in-groups and out-groups 24
Innovation Hub 7–18, 31, 37, 66
internal process minimisation 43
interpersonal issues 29–38, 110–111
Interview for a Role 131–133
interview-in-role 78, 101, 102, 128–129, 137–138, 141, 146
issue-at-the-centre method 92–95, 100

Kahneman, Daniel 77
Kim, W. 41f
kinaesthetic processing of information 99

Kitchen 12–13
knowledge, experiential versus propositional 118
Kross, E. 86

lateral thinking 16
Laundry 29–38
Lay it on the Table 53–66, 73
leadership reviews 121–125
leading in uncertainty 90
Lencioni, P. 112
length of time in each room 4
lines: as barrier/threshold 119–120; Living Report Card 110–125; Memory Lane 128–147; simple line methods 120–121 *see also* continuum line activities
Linsky, M. 68
live leadership reviews 121–125
Living Report Card 110–125
Living Room 89–108
looking 67–88
low hanging fruit 14
loyalties 71–77, 87

magnetic shapes 41–42, 71–73, 81–86, 91–95, 97–98
management/business speak 61, 99, 101, 102
matrix boxes 36, 41f, 49, 102, 103f
Mauborgne, R. 41f
memory 45, 97, 107, 118, 127–147
Memory Lane 128–147
mergers 138–141
mood 3
Moral-High-Ground 46
Moreno, J. 119
Moser, M. 107

Naïve Inquirer 59, 132
narcissistic injury 45
narratives 22–23, 53, 64–66, 110, 136, 142, 147
networks of relationships 70–71
neuroscience 8, 46, 83, 96, 107, 118
neutrality (of consultant) 132–133, 147
Niediek, J. 107
note-taker role 34
novelty/new information 8
number of visits per day 4
numbers of people in a Room 10

observation 4, 69, 73
organisational charts 71–73
organisational processes, minimisation of 43
Osborn, Alex 16
overview 67–88
ownership, sense of 11

Palmer, S. 98
Parkes, S. 92
peer consultation 90–99
Perry, C. 96
personal immersion 11
personification of abstract ideas 100–101
perspective 67–88
physical activities: advantages of 42, 95, 118–119; Lay it on the Table 53–66; Living Report Card 110–125; SWOT analysis 102–103 see also continuum line activities; drama-like activities; lines
physical representation of ideas 99–108
pillars 20, 21–27, 73
'pitching' sessions 11, 18
place and 'placeness' 107–108
plain language, benefits of 102
pooling ideas 11
Post-it notes 33, 100, 111–112, 114–115, 118, 119
PowerPoints 23, 97
pragmatics 9–10
privacy 5, 90
productivity as a business plan 8
projective techniques 56, 59
propositional versus experiential knowledge 118
pruning 14
Psychodrama 119, 121, 129
psychology: Attic 128, 132, 138, 146; Balcony 71, 73, 85; Basement 24; Dining Room 56; Living Room 107; Toilet 46, 47

Raise, Create, Eliminate, Reduce grid 41–42
red tape, reduction of 43
reductions/eliminations (Toilet) 39–51
redundancies 82
reflect-and-repair sessions 119
reform 29–38
regret avoidance 46, 50

regulation 44–45, 46–47
relationships 69, 71–88 see also Laundry
Relph, E. 108
remembering 127–147
repurposing rooms 149
restrictions, benefits of 3
retreats 40, 41, 44
'right' and 'left' brain 83, 118
Ringmaster role 127–128, 146
role-based interviews 78, 101, 102, 128, 131–133, 137–138, 141, 146
role reversal 77–79, 100–101
rooms (real) for working in 9–10, 129
routinisation 7

self-distancing 73, 79, 81, 86
self-transcendent viewpoints 73, 87
senior management: Balcony 67–88; peer consultation 90–99; 'pitching' to 11, 18; and the Toilet Room 44, 49–50
shapes, organisational 104–105
shared vision 23–24, 54
skills repertoires 87
snowball sampling 70, 79
social evolutionary perspectives 47
sociometrics: Balcony 70, 74, 75, 77; Dining Room 54; Living Report Card 119; Living Room 95
sorting laundry exercise 30–38
spatial methods 25 see also continuum line activities; lines; magnetic shapes
spokes-and-hub 74
stage (theatre-like) 4, 22–23, 73, 123
stages (theatre-like) 48, 73
stakeholder analysis 74
standing: Attic 130; Basement 25, 73; Innovation Hub 22; Laundry 35–36; Living Room 100, 104, 107; Memory Lane (Attic) 135, 136, 140; Study 114–116, 118–119, 123, 124 see also continuum line activities; lines
status quo bias 44, 45–46, 50, 76
stools and chairs 103–107, 143
strategy 39–40, 95
Study 109–125
suppliers 14, 66
support 19–27
SWOT analysis 102–103
systems views 67–88, 90, 110

team communication process 30
team issues 29–38, 110–111, 138–141
termites 23–24, 26–27
'thinking outside the box' 9
time-based activities 128–129
Toilet 31, 39–51
transformation 12–13
Treadwell, T. 119
tuning 71–77, 79–81, 85, 87

understanding 89–108

value propositions 23
vision 53–66
visual activities: Balcony 71–77, 81–86; Basement 22–23, 25–26; Dining Room 66; Living Report Card 110–125; Living Room 96–97; peer consultation 91–92 *see also* continuum line activities; lines; magnetic shapes
visual spaces 22–23, 25–26
Vitality 49, 53, 100, 103, 109–110, 118

wallpaper 40, 43
warm-ups: Basement 21; Innovation Hub 10, 11; Laundry 30; Living Room 91; Toilet 41
white ants 23–24, 26–27
Williams, A. 25, 143